Start, Run, and Profit from Your Own Home-Based Business

Start, Run, and Profit from Your Own Home-Based Business

A Revised Edition of
Dollars on Your Doorstep

Gregory Kishel
Patricia Kishel

WILEY

JOHN WILEY & SONS, INC.
New York • Chichester • Brisbane • Toronto • Singapore

A revised edition of *Dollars on Your Doorstep*, published by
John Wiley & Sons, Inc., in 1984.

Library of Congress Cataloging-in-Publication Data

Kishel, Gregory F., 1946–
    Start, run, and profit from your own home-based business /
Gregory F. Kishel, Patricia Gunter Kishel.
        p.   cm.
    Includes bibliographical references.
    ISBN 0-471-52588-X (C). — ISBN 0-471-52587-1 (P)
    1. Home-based businesses.   2. New business enterprises.
I. Kishel, Patricia Gunter, 1948–   . II. Title.
HD62.7.K582   1990
658'.041—dc20   90-12590
                                                           CIP

Printed in the United States of America

Preface

Start, Run, and Profit from Your Own Home-Based Business is written for the growing number of individuals who are choosing to work at home. An all-in-one guide for achieving business success, it is designed to help you turn part of your home into a thriving business. Step by step, it goes into every detail of setting up and furnishing your business, allocating time for it, protecting it, finding customers, and ultimately getting the sale.

As management consultants and business writers, we have had the opportunity to speak to home-based entrepreneurs and "telecommuters" (employees who work at home) throughout the United States. In so doing, we have discovered a real need for information specifically geared to the home-based businessperson—not just what it's like to work out of your home, but *how* to do it. This book provides that information. After reading it, you will know what to do, where to go, and whom to contact to get your business going and *keep* it going.

Among the questions you'll find answered in the following chapters are:

- What are the benefits of working at home?
- Which home-based business or occupation is right for me?

- How can I get started?
- What kinds of licenses or permits do I need?
- Where can I go to raise money for the business?
- What's the best way to market my products or services?
- How can I capitalize on free publicity?
- How do I handle taxes and insurance?
- What computer equipment and software should I buy?
- How can I juggle the needs of my family *and* the business?

In addition to this information, a *Tips* section at the end of each chapter will help you to carry out your plans and avoid costly mistakes. You'll also find a list of over 200 businesses and occupations that are particularly suited to a home-based setting, a daily time log and planner, and samples of the forms you are most likely to need.

To further ensure your success, all of Chapter 13, "Resources," is devoted to the books, directories, magazines, and associations you can turn to for help in your particular field.

Whether your home-based business is still in the idea stage or already up and running, you'll find the answers you need to profit at home.

Contents

1

The Benefits of Working at Home

HOME-BASED businesses, once made nearly extinct by the Industrial Revolution, are suddenly being called the growth industry of the future. Government and industry reports show that increasing numbers of men and women are now opting to work out of their homes. In a reversal of the nineteenth-century migration to huge factories and multilevel office complexes, entrepreneurs and employees alike are rediscovering the benefits of working at home.

Ever-lengthening commuting times, rising transportation costs, and changing lifestyles (the desire to combine a career and a family, or simply to escape the daily rat race) are part of the reason. Other factors include the continuing expansion of the services and information sectors and the widespread availability of microcomputers and fax machines—developments that have opened the door on a broad array of new home-based occupations. Add in the financial rewards, tax benefits, and more, and it's plain to see that it pays to work at home.

PERSONAL FREEDOM

The ability to gain control over one's life is perhaps the most enticing aspect of a home-based business. Rather than

bending to the demands of the work environment, individuals can mold their environments to meet their own
needs. Leaving behind time clocks, set routines, and work
spaces that are frequently impersonal or even hostile,
home-based workers have the freedom to earn and create
as they choose, in the comfort and convenience of their
own homes.

Instead of adapting to a nine-to-five, 40-hour work week,
the home-based worker can choose from an unlimited variety of scheduling options. Night people, who don't really
begin to be productive until 5 P.M., can work evenings if
they prefer. Morning people can start at the crack of dawn
and then stop in the early afternoon, free to pursue other
interests. Those who want to can work through the weekend or take a Tuesday afternoon off. When an idea comes
to you, whether you're reading, fixing dinner, battling
crabgrass, or sleeping, you can follow it up immediately.
A trip to your office takes just seconds.

Time, all too often the enemy, becomes your ally, expanding or contracting to conform to specific work as-
signments. The pressure to finish up what you're doing
before closing time, or to look busy even when you're not,
is eliminated. As a home-based businessperson, you determine your own hours.

Home-based workers have greater control not only over
their time but over their environments as well. The pictures
on the wall, the color of the curtains, and the direction
your desk faces are all your decisions. You need not tol-
erate piped-in music, cigarette smoke, unpleasant co-workers, or a room that's too hot or too cold. Energy that was
previously wasted arguing over the thermostat switch can
now be rechanneled toward your own fulfillment.

FINANCIAL BENEFITS

The financial benefits of working at home are equally attractive. Instead of waiting for a boss to give you a raise
or promotion, the amount of money you can earn is di-

rectly related to your own performance. Whether your business provides your sole means of support or a secondary income, its earning potential is up to you. What's more, people who have been frequently shut out of the job market—homemakers, students, retirees, and the disabled, to name a few—can use their home business to create new income opportunities.

In addition to the money you can *earn* by working at home, there's the money you can *save*. The reductions in the cost of transportation, business lunches, wardrobe, and children's day care are cause for celebration.

Simply by eliminating the need to commute to and from work, the home-based worker stands to realize savings ranging from a few hundred to several thousand dollars a year. If you normally use public transportation, your savings will naturally be lower. However, if you are currently driving your own car each day, the savings can be considerable, including money saved on gasoline and oil, maintenance, parking, and insurance.

Business lunches—often hurried, unappetizing, and overpriced affairs—need no longer be mandatory daily occurrences. Along with these, say good-bye to the office bandits, more commonly known as vending machines, that take your money while giving nothing in return. Home-based businesspersons have the luxury of eating what they want when they want, as well as the satisfaction of knowing that they got their money's worth.

Working out of your home also gives you the freedom to dress as you choose, thus reducing your clothing costs by doing away with the need for a separate "work wardrobe." Unless your business is one that constantly requires you to present a professional look (doctor, attorney, consultant), casual clothes probably will be the rule. Blue jeans, warm-ups, or even a bathrobe may be your uniform of the day.

Children's day-care centers, a fact of modern life in single-parent families or those in which both parents work, can put a big dent in the family budget. When more than one child is enrolled, the cost may seem to escalate faster than the national debt. The need to work and the shortage of affordable centers make the child-care problem a very real one. The solution for many people is a home-based business. This enables parents to be with their children and still earn an income. Children receive the care they need, and the money that would otherwise be spent to provide it can be used to improve the family's overall standard of living. The benefits to all are obvious.

Another benefit of locating your business at home is readily apparent: the money you can save by not renting office space. Rent payments, in many cases the single largest expense in running a business, can be a major stumbling block to getting started. Even when the money for rent is available, the accompanying requirements for a security deposit, maintenance, and cleaning fees or the pressure to sign a long-term lease, can be overwhelming. Converting a portion of your home into work space enables you to avoid this, lowering both your costs and your risk.

TAX SAVINGS

Using your home as a place of business offers a number of tax advantages (see Chapter 10). For starters, it allows you to deduct a part of the operating and depreciation expenses on your home. This means that a percentage of your rent or mortgage payment, depreciation, property taxes, insurance, utilities, and expenses for household maintenance, repairs, or improvements is deductible.

The percentage you can deduct depends on the number of rooms or square feet of space that are set aside *regularly* and *exclusively* for business purposes. For instance, if you turn one room of a five-room apartment into an office, workroom, or storage area, you can deduct 20 percent of the apartment's overall operating expenses. In order to qualify for this deduction, you must use the space designated for your business on an ongoing basis solely for the purpose of conducting business. Space that you use for other activities, or only use infrequently, does not meet

Internal Revenue Service requirements and is therefore not deductible.

Another deduction you may be entitled to is the expense of using an automobile or other motor vehicle in your business. On the basis of the number of miles you drive the vehicle for business purposes, you can deduct a percentage of its upkeep and operating costs. Deductible expenses include gas, oil, repairs, insurance, depreciation, interest on car payments, taxes, licenses, garage rent, parking fees, and tolls.

The actual expense of running your business is also deductible. You can deduct the money you spend on supplies or postage, to purchase business cards, to take a client to lunch, attend professional seminars, promote your business, or to pay accounting fees. "To be deductible," the IRS states, "a business expense must be ordinary in your business and necessary for its operation." According to the IRS, "The word *ordinary* refers to an expense that is common and accepted practice in the industry. *Necessary* expenses are those that are appropriate and helpful in developing and maintaining your business." Thus, an expense that meets both parts of this test is deductible.

If you have a home-based business, the IRS requires that you separate your personal from your business expenses. Only the business expenses are deductible. To make sure that you receive the tax benefits to which you're entitled, it's a good idea to see a tax accountant.

FAMILY TOGETHERNESS

In many instances, home-based businesses are strengthening family relationships by enabling the whole family to get involved. Instead of going in separate directions, more and more husbands and wives are pooling their energies and working toward a common goal. At the same time, children have an opportunity to see what their parents do for a living . . . and to learn about business firsthand.

Pleased by her youngest son's initiative, one home-based entrepreneur we spoke with exclaimed, "Stevie told me that if I taught him how to do the sales demos, I'd never have to do them again! Working at home has really brought us all together."

The word "together" turns up frequently in conversations with home-based businesspersons. Often comparing themselves to the early settlers and pioneers, who built their own homes and worked out of them too, today's entrepreneurs place much emphasis on team effort. The family, united for a shared purpose, is able to work together to develop the business.

REDUCED STRESS

Electing to work out of your home can go a long way toward reducing stress, particularly the stress that comes from trying to juggle the demands of your work life with those of your private life. Instead of having to decide whether to go to work or stay at home when a child is ill, you can do both. Conversely, when you have to work late at night to complete a project, you can still take a break for dinner with your family and then resume work afterward.

Office politics and arguments among co-workers, two wellknown causes of stress, can be eliminated by working at home. Furthermore, there's no one to tell you when to punch in or punch out, take a break, go to lunch, turn in a report, or attend a meeting—decisions that were once made by others can now be made by you. The fear of being passed over for a promotion, denied a raise, laid off, or fired is no longer cause for anxiety.

A former television producer we know left broadcasting to start her own home-based media consulting firm. After being ruled by production schedules and all-day tapings, she was only too happy to escape the harsh lights and air conditioned chill of the television stations where she used to work.

Converting her front bedroom into a state-of-the-art studio where clients could rehearse for upcoming television appearances removed much of the pressure she was under.

It also eliminated the need to spend two or more hours on the freeway each day. As an added bonus, by basing the studio in her condominium she and her employees gained access to a swimming pool, a Jacuzzi, and an exercise room—stress-reducing amenities that otherwise would have been unavailable.

JOB ENRICHMENT

One of the benefits most frequently mentioned regarding home-based businesses is job enrichment. Unlike the typical worker, who is boxed into one job and given a label identifying him or her as a bookkeeper, plumber, attorney, manager, or secretary, the home-based businessperson is free to learn and perform a variety of work-related tasks. It's possible to go over your billings in the morning, use the remaining time until lunch to produce the product or service you provide, take care of phone calls and personal correspondence in the afternoon, and then wrap up the day by putting the finishing touches on the advertising copy for a new brochure. Not only is it possible, it's probable.

Working at home allows you to devote the entire day to one activity or to a succession of activities. Barring a specific deadline that has to be met, you can set one project aside if you want to, and focus on another. Then, when you're ready to resume work on the first project, you can pick it up again.

Varying your activities like this and working at a pace that's natural for you helps to ensure that you won't get bored. Instead of going through the motions of performing a task, there's a feeling of involvement. And, since everything you do is directed at making your business a success, you will experience a sense of excitement. Every time the phone rings represents a new opportunity.

Working in this fashion can't help but inspire a high level of creativity. After getting away from the tunnel vision found in so many organizations, home-based businesspersons develop an understanding of all aspects of their own businesses. This puts you in a better position to come up with improved methods of doing things. Duplicated procedures and wasted steps can be more readily spotted. What works in one area can possibly be applied in another.

By working at home you will also learn about yourself, in addition to learning a great deal about business in general and your own business in particular. What really interests you? What influences your decisions? What are your capabilities? "The personal growth has been fantastic," a teacher-turned-entrepreneur told us. "I've learned more in the last year than I learned in six years of college and all that living before. It really has been marvelous, absolutely super."

INCREASED PRODUCTIVITY

Home-based businesspersons generally agree that working at home helps them to be more productive. Part of the reason for this is that there's simply more time available. Hours that would normally be spent commuting can be used to run the business instead. Another reason that can't be overlooked is the increased level of enthusiasm on the part of home-based workers. Many get so caught up in what they're doing that it's actually hard for them to stop.

Speaking from our own experience, we've often worked through a weekend without even realizing it. The fact that we have the freedom to switch gears when we choose—to take a break, do something around the house, or whatever—keeps us from getting tired and makes what we're doing seem less like work.

COMPETITIVE ADVANTAGE

Working out of your home can enable you to be more competitive, not just in the prices you charge but also in the quality of service you offer. You can use the money you save on rent to increase your overall profitability, or you can pass it on to customers in the form of lower prices. Competitors restricted by higher overhead costs have no such options. What they charge is predetermined by their rental agreements. The higher the rent, the higher their prices.

Having your business in your home also makes it easier to provide customers with personal service. If someone needs to reach you in the evening or over the weekend, for example, you're there, ready to answer a question or supply the necessary information. What's more, when customers come to see you, they don't have to park in gargantuan parking structures or walk through crowded shopping centers. And, upon arriving, they can be welcomed into an atmosphere that is warm and inviting.

Given these benefits and more, the trend toward home-based businesses is clearly just beginning. Those who have recognized the opportunities existing under their own roofs are in the forefront of a growing movement. Spurred on by a need to be independent and the drive to succeed, others will continue to join their ranks.

The American dream of owning your own business, a dream thought by many to be unattainable, is not only within your sight but at your doorstep. You need look no farther than your kitchen, bedroom, den, living room, or garage to find the foundation on which to build your business enterprise.

2

Picking a Winner

MAKING the decision to start your own home-based business is one thing; knowing which type of business to start is another. In evaluating the various options, how can you be sure that the business you choose will enable you to reach your goals, both personally and professionally? In short, how can you tell if you've picked a winner?

There are no sure things in business, only possibilities. But, by taking certain factors into consideration, you can shift the odds in your favor. These factors include the economy, customer preferences, competitors, available resources, and even the political climate. The most important factor of all, though, is you. Picking a winner calls for you to look inward and to ask yourself "What do I really want to do?" Just because a business is right for your neighbor doesn't mean it will be right for you. To increase your chances of success, you should select a business that genuinely appeals to you.

TURNING YOUR INTERESTS INTO INCOME

Prospective entrepreneurs often make the mistake of narrowing their choices too quickly, starting the first business that comes to mind. Instead of stumbling into this pitfall, try to expand your choices and come up with ideas for business that you would actually *enjoy* running. The object is to discover those business opportunities that should be not only profitable but personally satisfying as well. As shown in the Guide for Turning Your Interests into Income, the trick is to match the business to your preferences, rather than vice versa.

GUIDE FOR TURNING YOUR INTERESTS INTO INCOME

1. Write down all of your interests, hobbies, leisure activities, and previous work or volunteer experiences that you have enjoyed. (For example, traveling, collecting miniature furniture, cooking, shopping, fishing, working with computers, meeting people.)

   _____   _____   _____

   _____   _____   _____

   _____   _____   _____

2. The next step is to convert your interests into income opportunities. (For example, if you like to ski and travel, you might want to organize ski charters; or, if you're interested in photography and enjoy meeting people, perhaps a videotaping service would be right for you.)

   _____   _____

   _____   _____

   _____   _____

3. Now, narrow the list down to the three or four businesses that appeal to you the most:

   _____   _____

   _____   _____

4. Research these further to determine which is your best bet. (For example, who would your customers be? How can you reach them? Who's your competition? How much money will you need to get started?) The rest is up to you.

Once you've completed the Guide's four steps, you may be surprised by the results. A business that originally seemed like a good idea might not show up on your list. Conversely, an activity you've always done purely for fun could emerge as a potential money-maker.

When you're researching the final choices, don't forget to take your own qualifications into consideration. For instance, if a proposed business will require that you have frequent personal contact with others, do you have the necessary human-relations and communications skills? Or, given the various functions to be performed, how strong is your technical ability? The amount of time you're willing to put into your home-based business and the degree of risk you feel comfortable with must also be weighed carefully.

PHYSICAL CHARACTERISTICS

In choosing a home-based business, you should pay special attention to the physical characteristics of the enterprise. How much space will it take up? What equipment will you need? Is the business safe? Does it generate pollution? Does it conform to local zoning restrictions? Based on your answers to these questions, you may determine that a particular business simply isn't adaptable to your present location or, for that matter, to any home setting.

Space

Whereas one business might require only occasional space on your kitchen table, another could easily spread out to fill every available room and closet. To avoid being squeezed out of your home, you should estimate the space requirements of your intended business in advance. If you have very little space to allocate to the business, this consideration is critical. Service businesses such as tutoring, videotaping, housecleaning, or resume preparation generally take up the least amount of space. This is because they tend to have less inventory and equipment than retailing or manufacturing businesses. Thus, if you are planning to enter the import-export field (retailing) or design custom T-shirts (manufacturing), you will need more storage and work space.

To estimate the amount of space your business will need, draw a layout depicting the physical arrangement of the furniture, equipment, supplies, and merchandise you will need to operate your enterprise. In this way you can see, at least on paper, how the business fits into your home. You can experiment with different arrangements until you find the layout that works best.

Equipment

As far as the equipment to be used in your business is concerned, the amount of space it takes up is just one of the things to consider. Others include the equipment's weight, energy consumption, operating temperatures, noise levels, ventilation requirements, and safety features. For example, equipment that is very heavy can cause structural damage to floors, walls, or ceilings. If it consumes a great deal of electricity or generates extreme heat, equipment can also overload electrical circuits or even cause a fire. Computers and other electronic equipment such as modems and fax machines must have proper ventilation and must be kept out of direct sunlight.

Safety

To protect the health and well-being of those who come into contact with your business, you must ensure that it meets high safety standards. This particularly applies when children are present. Thus, a business that would be acceptable in another location could be unsuitable when based in the home. In determining just how safe a business is, it's often helpful to talk to an insurance agent. An agent can point out what things to look for and tell you whether or not insurance that specifically covers the business is necessary. Even if you already have homeowner's or renter's insurance, you may find that you need additional coverage since standard policies frequently exclude home-based businesses.

Pollution

For obvious reasons, the less pollution associated with your home-based business the better. This refers to all kinds of pollution, not just the two most common ones—air and water pollution. In this regard, you should also rate the business in terms of noise pollution and visual pollution. Is it relatively quiet to operate? Is it visually appealing to others? A tap-dancing studio in an upstairs apartment or an automobile body repair shop next door to a neighbor's garden would both get poor ratings.

Zoning

Zoning restrictions established by each community usually set forth guidelines for using one's home as a place of business. Those things typically regulated include the types of business that are acceptable, size and placement of signs, hours of operation, and the number of parking spaces permitted. Depending on the community, one home-based business might conform to local zoning restrictions while another quite similar one doesn't. For example, one city allows psychiatrists to work at home but doesn't extend the same right to psychologists. Another city limits the size of home-based businesses, prohibiting them from taking up more than 25 percent of the space in the housing units they occupy. For additional information on the impact that zoning restrictions can have on your home-based business, check Chapter 3.

ORGANIZATIONAL CHARACTERISTICS

In addition to focusing on the physical characteristics of your business, you should also pay attention to its organizational characteristics. How many people will you need to run it? Will customers come to you or will you go to them? How are you going to reach suppliers? What role, if any, will family members play in the business? Here you want to find the business whose organizational characteristics are most in sync with your needs and those of your family.

Workers

The number of people who will be employed in your business is a major consideration from both a practical standpoint and a psychological one. Practically speaking, there are the problems of available space, working conditions, and overhead costs. Psychologically, you must deal with such issues as privacy and the need to establish satisfactory work relationships. Given limited space or the desire to maintain your privacy, a business that you can run by yourself or solely with the aid of family members is the answer. In contrast to this, if you don't like working alone or are afraid that a home-based business would isolate you, then a business that employs others is a better choice.

Customers

Some home-based businesses require little or no personal contact with customers. In mail-order sales, for instance, orders come in and packages go out. But, in the majority of businesses, entrepreneur and customer ultimately do come face to face. You can accomplish this by having customers come to you, or you can go to them. Each method has its advantages. Having customers come to you reduces the time and money you would otherwise spend commuting. And, if you have children to care for, this will enable you to stay at home with them. On the other hand, by going out to the customer, you eliminate the need to maintain a showroom or an elaborate office. Entrepreneurs who charge an hourly rate for their services sometimes find that this also makes it easier to keep appointments from running beyond their allotted times; when a meeting is over, rather than waiting for the customer to leave, the entrepreneur is the one who goes.

Suppliers

The type of business you select and your location will have a direct bearing on your ability to obtain supplies and merchandise. For example, gift items are often introduced at trade shows and craft fairs held in various parts of the country. To obtain clothing and fashion accessories, entrepreneurs are likely to travel to New York, Los Angeles, or Dallas where many of the major manufacturers in the garment industry have their outlets. In both cases, you would need to calculate the travel costs involved and the time spent away from home. Since these can be prohibitive, it's fortunate that there are other ways to get in touch with suppliers.

In many industries—food services, for one—the normal procedure is to employ sales representatives to call on customers. This does away with the need for you to travel, but still means setting aside time to talk to representatives when they are in your area. The easiest ways to order supplies and merchandise, particularly if your business is in a remote location, are by mail and by telephone. These are the most convenient because you don't have to set up sales appointments or leave your home.

Family

The role of family members in a home-based business is always an important one, whether or not they actually participate in the activities of the business. The more enthusiastically they support your business venture, the more likely it is to succeed. Thus, throughout the process of choosing a business and going through the steps to make it operational, you should consult your family. Rather than expect family members to accept the business on an "as is" basis, it's better to solicit their ideas and suggestions from the start. This way, they will not only feel more positive about the business, but will be more inclined to lend a hand when you need help.

TYPES OF HOME-BASED BUSINESSES AND OCCUPATIONS

Those businesses that are best suited to a home location are able to exist in the midst of family members and neighbors without offending either group. Most home-based businesses don't require a great deal of space or utilize heavy machinery. And, more often than not, the owner of the business can run it alone or with a minimum amount of outside help. Aside from this, though, each home-based business is different, reflecting the individual needs and preferences of its owner and conforming to the demands of its environment.

Some of the following businesses and occupations have proven to be particularly successful in home settings.

A

Accountant
Acting Instructor
Acupuncturist
Advertising Agency
Agricultural Consultant
Animal Boarding and
    Shipping
Animal Trainer
Answering Service
Antique Appraiser
Antique Shop
Architect
Art Broker
Artist
Arts and Crafts Sales
Astrologer
Attorney
Auctioneer
Auditor

B

Baby-sitter
Bail Bondsman
Bait and Tackle Sales
Baker
Balloon Bouquets
Barber
Bartending Instructor
Beauty Consultant
Bed and Breakfast
Beekeeper
Billing Service
Bookkeeper
Book Publicist
Book Publisher

Boutique
Broadcaster
Broker
Bus Charter
Buyer

C

Cake Baking
Cake Decorating
Calligrapher
Campaign Advisor
Career Counselor
Carpenter
Carpet Cleaner
Cartoonist
Caterer
Chauffeur
Chiropractor
Cleaning Service
Clipping Bureau
Clothing Sales
Clown
Collection Agency
Color Consultant
Communications
   Consultant
Computer Dating
Computer Software
   Design
Computer Specialist
Convalescent Home
Copywriter
Counselor

D

Dance Instructor
Data Processor

Day-Care Center
Delivery Service
Dental Technician
Dentist
Desktop Publishing
Doctor
Doll Hospital
Draftsman
Driving Instructor

E

Editor
Electronic Repair
Employment Agency
Engineer
Engraver
Escrow Service
Event/Party Planner
Eviction Service
Exercise Salon
Exporter
Exterminator

F

Fashion Designer
Financial Consultant
Fire Adjuster
Florist
Fund-raiser
Furniture Repair

G

Gardener
Genealogist
Gift Basket Service
Gift Shop

Glass Blowing
Gourmet Cooking School
Gourmet Foods
Graphic Designer

H

Hair Stylist
Handwriting Expert
Handyman
Health Food Store
Herb Farming
House Painter

I J K

Illustrator
Image Consultant
Importer
Income Tax Preparation
Information Broker
Instructor
Insurance Agent
Interior Designer
Inventor
Jewelerymaker
Knitting

L

Landscape Architect
Lecture Bureau
Legal Researcher
Locksmith

M

Magician
Mailbox Rental

Mail Order
Management Consultant
Manicurist
Manufacturer's Agent
Marketing Consultant
Martial Arts Instructor
Massage
Mechanic
Media Consultant
Modeling School
Movie Producer
Moving Service
Music Teacher
Musician

N O P

Newsletter Publisher
Nurse
Nutritionist
Office Planning Service
Palmist
Paralegal Service
Patternmaker
Personal Organizer
Personal Shopping Service
Pet Grooming
Photographer
Picnic Basket Sales
Picture Framing
Plumber
Pollster
Pool Cleaning Service
Press Agent
Printer
Private Investigator
Public Relations
Puppeteer
Purchasing Agent

Q

Quit Smoking Clinic

R

Reading Specialist
Real Estate Sales
Recording Studio
Researcher
Restaurant
Résumé Service
Rock Shop
Roommate Bureau

S

Salesperson
Sandwich Sales
School
Screen Printing
Script Typing Service
Seamstress
Security Specialist
Seminars
Shoe Repair
Solar Energy Consultant
Souvenir Shop
Speaker
Sports Promoter
Stockbroker
Surveyor

T

Tailor
Taxidermist
Telemarketing
Therapist
Tour Operator
Translator
Travel Agent
T-Shirt Shop
Tutoring
Typesetter
Talent Agent

U V W

Undertaker
Urban Planner
Videotaping Service
Wake-Up Call Service
Watch Repair
Wedding Consultant
Weight-Loss Clinic
Welcome Wagon
Window Cleaner
Word Processing
Writer

X Y Z

Yarn Shop

BUSINESS SELECTION TIPS

1. Instead of choosing the first business that comes to mind, take the time to explore your various options.
2. Use the Guide for Turning Your Interests into Income

to find out what type of business appeals to you the most.

3. Choose a business that will be personally satisfying as well as profitable.
4. Draw a layout of your intended work area to see how it will fit into its allotted space in your home.
5. Make sure the business meets high safety standards, especially if you have children at home.
6. Check with an insurance agent to determine what kind of insurance coverage the business is going to need.
7. Find out in advance whether or not the business complies with local zoning ordinances.
8. For the sake of your family and neighbors, pick a business that is relatively pollution-free.
9. Select a business whose organizational characteristics are compatible with your needs and those of your family.
10. Get family members involved in the business from the very beginning while it is still in the planning stage.

3

Living with the Law

ONCE you've selected the type of business that's right for you, the next step is to take appropriate action to keep your business legal. This is as much for your own protection as for the public's, since it gives your business a recognizable and legitimate standing in the community. Thus, to make sure that you are starting your home-based business off on the right foot, it's a good idea to pay a visit to City Hall.

Depending on what you sell and where you live, different licenses, permits, or other paperwork may be required. The following should help you to determine which local, state, and federal regulations apply to your business. Along with this, the section on choosing a legal structure is intended to make your business run more smoothly.

LOCAL REGULATIONS

At the local level, regulations pertaining to home-based businesses are primarily concerned with taxation, public health and safety, and zoning. Although each community is different, the most typical forms of regulation are described here.

Business Tax and Permit

In order to operate a business out of your home, you may have to obtain a business tax and permit, commonly referred to as a *business license*. This is usually issued by the city and/or county in which a business is located and is valid for one to two years. The fee for it is based on the gross sales of your business and can range from less than $50 to more than $100. In many instances, though, home-based businesses are charged a reduced rate. To contact the agency that issues business permits in your area, check the White Pages of your telephone directory under City of _____, Business Tax Division, Business Licenses, Licenses, or City Clerk.

Fictitious Business Name Statement

If your surname is not included in the name of your business (Sandy's Doll Repair, Midtown Realty Co., J&M Services), then you will probably need to file a fictitious business name statement with the county clerk's office. The purpose of this statement is to protect consumers by making available to the public your identity and the identities of any others who are co-owners with you in the business. For example, a ficitious name statement would generally be required in each of these instances:

- When the business name doesn't include the surname of each owner
- When the business name itself suggests the existence of additional owners unknown to the public (Company, and Sons, and Associates, Brothers)
- When the business name (if it is a corporation) is not stated in the articles of incorporation

In the event that it is necessary to file a fictitious name statement, this should usually be done within forty days after the business commences operations. A two-part process, this involves (1) filing the statement with the county clerk, and (2) having the statement published in a news-

A MAIL CERTIFIED COPIES TO:	B PUBLISH IN NEWSPAPER:
NAME _____	COUNTY CLERK'S FILING STAMP
ADDRESS _____	
CITY _____	

FICTITIOUS BUSINESS NAME STATEMENT

THE FOLLOWING PERSON(S) IS (ARE) DOING BUSINESS AS:

1: Fictitious Business Name (s)

2: Street Address, City & State of Principal place of Business in California   Zip Code

3.

Full Name of Registrant	Full Name of Registrant
Residence Address	Residence Address
City State Zip	City State Zip
(if corporation, show state of incorporation)	(if corporation, show state of incorporation)
Full Name of Registrant	Full Name of Registrant
Residence Address	Residence Address
City State Zip	City State Zip
(if corporation, show state of incorporation)	(if corporation, show state of incorporation)

4. This business is conducted by ( )an individual,   ( ) individuals (Husband & Wife),   ( ) a general partnership,   ( ) a limited partnership
( ) an unincorporated association other than a partnership,   ( ) a corporation,   ( ) a business trust   (CHECK ONE ONLY)

5A.

Signed _____

Typed or Printed _____

5B. If Registrant a corporation sign below:

Corporation Name _____

Signature & Title _____

Type or Print
Officer's Name & Title _____

This statement was filed with the County Clerk of _____ County on date indicated by file stamp above.

6. New Fictitious Business Name Statement ☐

File No. _____

7. Refile — Statement expires December 31. ☐

I HEREBY CERTIFY THAT THIS COPY IS A CORRECT COPY OF THE ORIGINAL STATEMENT ON FILE IN MY OFFICE.

_____
COUNTY CLERK

BY _____ DEPUTY

File No. _____

CALIFORNIA NEWSPAPER SERVICE BUREAU, Inc. P.O. BOX 31, LOS ANGELES, CALIFORNIA 90053

LOS ANGELES	SACRAMENTO	SAN DIEGO	SAN FRANCISCO	SANTA ANA
(213) 625-2541	(916) 444-3950	(714) 232-0408	(415) 391-6616	(714) 547-4844

FILE WITH COUNTY CLERK

A FICTITIOUS BUSINESS NAME STATEMENT.

paper of general circulation. The second part is to ensure that the public has an opportunity to see your statement. To save time and simplify the process, instead of going to the county clerk's office first, go directly to the newspaper where your statement will appear. Most newspapers carry fictitious name forms as a convenience to their customers and will not only file the completed statement for you, but will assist you in filling it out. The total cost for filing and publishing the statement should be somewhere between $30 and $90.

Zoning Restrictions

Just as some people are more entrepreneurially inclined than others, so are some communities. Whereas one neighborhood might welcome the presence of your home-based business, another neighborhood might object to it. Some communities do not permit home-based businesses to post signs or have exterior merchandise displays. There also may be zoning restrictions limiting the number of employees you can hire or the acceptable level of customer traffic to your door. Since the main purpose of zoning restrictions is to protect the rights of people and property, a business that is noisy, smelly, or unsightly can expect to run into trouble. In general, though, most home-based businesses—particularly non-polluting, low-profile enterprises—manage to operate alongside their neighbors without incident. To find out what zoning restrictions, if any, will affect your business, contact the planning department for your city or township.

Other Regulations

Depending on the nature of your business, other local regulations may also apply. For instance, if you are engaged in food preparation, processing, or serving (mail-order cheesecakes, bottled salad dressing, catering), you must stay within the county health department codes. Antique dealers often find that a permit from the police department is a prerequisite for doing business. Other departments that have jurisdiction over home-based businesses include the fire and sanitation departments.

STATE REGULATIONS

At the state level, regulations pertaining to home-based businesses center around taxation and the monitoring of specific professions. Each state sets its own standards in these areas, but the most common regulations involve the issuing of seller's permits and state licenses.

Seller's Permit

If your business buys and sells merchandise and you live in a state that taxes retail sales, then it is likely that you will need a seller's permit. This permit (1) exempts you from paying sales tax on the merchandise you purchase from suppliers for resale through your business, and (2) authorizes you to collect sales tax from your customers. Moreover, in states that require a seller's permit, you may need one to be admitted to trade shows or to purchase goods at wholesale prices.

Usually there is no fee to obtain a seller's permit, but, depending on your estimated gross sales for the year, you may be required to post a bond. This is to ensure that you collect and remit to the state all sales taxes due. To find out more about the seller's permit and whether or not you should have one, check your telephone directory White Pages under "State of _____ Taxes."

State Licenses

As a means of protecting the consumer, most states regulate entry into specific occupations. Thus, in order to operate certain kinds of home-based businesses, you may be required to have a license. To obtain one, you will need to meet the standards of ability and professionalism set forth by the state licensing agency that has jurisdiction over your industry. Once issued, a license is usually valid for a period of one to two years, at which time it must be renewed.

Businesspersons who generally require state licenses to operate include:

Accountants
Architects
Barbers
Contractors
Cosmetologists
Dental Hygienists
Dentists
Electronic Repair Persons
Employment Agents
Engineers
Insurance Adjusters

Manicurists
Marriage Counselors
Opticians
Physical Therapists
Physicians
Podiatrists
Psychologists
Real Estate Brokers
Shorthand Reporters
Social Workers
Veterinarians

To find out which state licensing agency, if any, has jurisdiction over your business, check the telephone directory White Pages under "State of _____," and the specific vocation.

FEDERAL REGULATIONS

At the federal level, regulations pertaining to home-based businesses focus on taxation, employer responsibilities, consumer protection, and the registration of trademarks, patents, and copyrights.

Employer Identification Number

If you employ one or more persons in your business, the federal government requires you to have an employer identification number. This enables the government to verify that you are paying all appropriate employer taxes and withholding the proper amounts from employee paychecks. You can obtain an employer identification number by filling out IRS form number SS-4 and submitting it to the Internal Revenue Service. There is no fee for this.

Form **SS-4** (Rev. August 1988) Department of the Treasury Internal Revenue Service	**Application for Employer Identification Number** (For use by employers and others. Please read the attached Instructions before completing this form.) Please type or print clearly.	Offical Use Only OMB No. 1545-0003 Expires 7-31-91

1 Name of applicant (True legal name. See instructions.)

2 Trade name of business if different from item 1 | **3** Executor, trustee, "care of name"

4 Mailing address (street address) (room, apt., or suite no.) | **5** Address of business, if different from item 4. (See instructions.)

4a City, state, and ZIP code | **5a** City, state, and ZIP code

6 County and State where principal business is located

7 Name of principal officer, grantor, or general partner. (See instructions.) ►

8 Type of entity (Check only one.) (See instructions.)
- ☐ Individual SSN
- ☐ REMIC   ☐ Personal service corp.
- ☐ State/local government   ☐ National guard
- ☐ Other nonprofit organization (specify)
- ☐ Farmers' cooperative
- ☐ Estate   ☐ Trust
- ☐ Other (specify) ►
- ☐ Plan administrator SSN
- ☐ Other corporation (specify)
- ☐ Federal government/military
- ☐ Partnership
- ☐ Church or church controlled organization

If nonprofit organization enter GEN (if applicable)

8a If a corporation, give name of foreign country (if applicable) or state in the U.S. where incorporated ► | Foreign country | State

9 Reason for applying (check only one)
- ☐ Started new business
- ☐ Hired employees
- ☐ Created a pension plan (specify type) ►
- ☐ Banking purpose (specify) ►
- ☐ Changed type of organization (spec fy) ►
- ☐ Purchased going business
- ☐ Created a trust (specify) ►
- ☐ Other (specify) ►

10 Business start date or acquisition date (Mo., day, year) (See instructions.) | **11** Enter closing month of accounting year (See instructions.)

12 First date wages or annuities were paid or will be paid (Mo., day, year). Note: *If applicant is a withholding agent, enter date income will first be paid to nonresident alien. (Mo., day, year).* . . . . ►

13 Enter highest number of employees expected in the next 12 months. Note: *If the applicant does not expect to have any employees during the period, enter "0.".* . . . . ► | Nonagricultural | Agricultural | Household

14 Does the applicant operate more than one place of business? . . . . ☐ Yes ☐ No
If "Yes," enter name of business. ►

15 Principal activity or service (See instructions.) ►

16 Is the principal business activity manufacturing?. . . . . ☐ Yes ☐ No
If "Yes," principal product and raw material used. ►

17 To whom are most of the products or services sold? Please check the appropriate box.   ☐ Business (wholesale)
☐ Public (retail)   ☐ Other (specify) ►   ☐ N/A

18 Has the applicant ever applied for an identification number for this or any other business?. . . . . ☐ Yes ☐ No
Note: *If "Yes," please answer items 18a and 18b.*

18a If the answer to item 18 is "Yes," give applicant's true name and trade name, if different when applicant applied.

True name ►   Trade name ►

18b Enter approximate date, city, and state where the application was filed and the previous employer identification number if known.

Approximate date when filed (Mo., day, year) | City, and state where filed | Previous EIN

Under penalties of perjury, I declare that I have examined this application, and to the best of my knowledge and belief, it is true, correct, and complete. | Telephone number (include area code)

Name and title (please type or print clearly) ►

Signature ►   Date ►

Note: *Do not write below this line.   For official use only.*

Please leave blank ►	Geo.	Ind.	Class	Reason for applying

For Paperwork Reduction Act Notice, see Instructions.   ☆U.S. Government Printing Office: 1988-523-133/00332   Form **SS-4** (Rev. 8-88)

FORM NUMBER SS-4 APPLICATION FOR
EMPLOYER IDENTIFICATION NUMBER.

At the same time, you should ask the IRS for its free publication number 454, *Your Business Tax Kit*. This contains tax instructions, forms, sample notices sent to businesses, a checklist, and calendar of due dates for filing returns and paying taxes. Both the SS-4 form and the business tax kit are available at your local IRS office. To locate the office closest to you, check your telephone directory White Pages under "United States Government Office—Internal Revenue Service."

Consumer Protection Regulation

To protect the rights of consumers, the federal government regulates business practices in a variety of areas. Home-based businesses that engage in mail-order sales, interstate commerce, or the import-export trade, for example, are subject to regulation by one or more of these agencies: Federal Trade Commission, Interstate Commerce Commission, U.S. Postal Service, U.S. Custom Service. The Federal Trade Commission also oversees product packaging and labeling, product warranties, and the manufacturing and labeling of textiles, fabrics, and articles of clothing. To familiarize yourself with the regulations that apply to your type of business, you should write to the Federal Trade Commission Washington, D.C. 20580. The FTC can provide the information you need and also tell you which other agencies to contact should it be necessary.

Trademarks, Patents, and Copyrights

In addition to protecting the rights of consumers, the federal government also protects the rights of entrepreneurs. In this case, it protects your right to use and profit from your own name (or business or product name), inventions, and artistic creations. Before you can take full advantage of this right, though, you must be aware of the government regulations that apply to trademarks, patents, and copyrights.

Trademarks

A trademark (or service mark) is any word, name, symbol, device, or combination of these used to identify the products or services of a business and to distinguish them from those of other enterprises. The trademark can be one of the most valuable assets of a business, helping to define its image, increase customer recognition, and stimulate repeat purchases. One has only to think of McDonald's golden arches, the Xerox name, or the distinctive Coca-Cola bottle to realize the advantage of having a strong trademark. Given this, it's in your own best interest to create a trademark for your business, then take appropriate steps to safeguard it.

In creating a trademark, it helps to follow these basic rules:

- Keep the name simple, short, and easy to pronounce.
- Choose a design or symbol that is distinctive and easily recognizable.
- Make sure that the trademark has positive connotations both in the United States and abroad.
- Avoid using your surname alone as your trademark because anyone else with the same name can also use it.
- Avoid trademarks that are merely descriptive (Fast Service) or geographic (Texas Chili). Since others can rightfully use them too, the government doesn't consider these legitimate trademarks.
- Avoid using a trademark that is misleading or confusingly similar to an existing trademark.

Although you can legally use a trademark without registering it, this is not advisable. To safeguard your trademark, you should register it with the U.S. Patent and Trademark Office. (See application form on pages 32 and 33.) This helps to not only strengthen your claim to the trademark but also to establish the date on which you first began using it. Once your trademark is registered, your right to use it extends for a period of ten years, at which time registration is renewable. For more information on trademarks and procedures, write to the U.S. Department of Commerce, Patent and Trademark Office, Washington, D.C. 20231.

Patents

In granting a patent to an inventor, the federal government gives him or her the right to exclude all others from making, using, or selling the patented invention in the United States. Patents for new and useful products or processes are valid for a period of 17 years from the date of issuance. A design patent, covering only the style or appearance of a product, may be valid 3½, 7, or 14 years, as specified in the patent application.

If you develop a product, process, or design you believe has commercial possibilities, obtaining a patent may be advisable, given the protection it affords. The government recommends that inventors not attempt to prepare their own patent applications without the help of a registered attorney or agent skilled in patent procedures. Taking this into consideration, when legal fees are added in, the total cost of obtaining a patent usually runs between $2,000 and $5,000.

To protect your claim to an invention prior to the issuance of a patent, be sure to follow these guidelines:

1. Keep good records detailing the progress of your invention from the idea stage to its final form. These should be in ink, signed and dated by you, and witnessed by someone other than a co-inventor.
2. Conduct a search to discover if any inventions identical or similar to yours have already been patented. Your findings here will, to a great extent, determine whether or not you should apply for a patent.
3. Utilize the services of a patent attorney or agent if you decide to go ahead and file a patent application.
4. Don't jeopardize your right to your own invention. This will occur if, more than one year prior to filing the patent application, you (1) publicly use or sell the invention, or (2) allow information about it to be printed

TRADEMARK APPLICATION, PRINCIPAL REGISTER, WITH DECLARATION (Partnership)	MARK *(identify the mark)*
	CLASS NO. *(if known)*

TO THE COMMISSIONER OF PATENTS AND TRADEMARKS:

NAME OF PARTNERSHIP

NAMES OF PARTNERS

BUSINESS ADDRESS OF PARTNERSHIP

CITIZENSHIP OF PARTNERS

The above identified applicant has adopted and is using the trademark shown in the accompanying drawing[1] for the following goods: _____

_____ .

and requests that said mark be registered in the United States Patent and Trademark Office on the Principal Register established by the Act of July 5, 1946.

The trademark was first used on the goods[2] on _____ ; was first used on the goods[2] in
 (date)

_____ commerce[3] on _____ ; and is now in use in
 (type of commerce) *(date)*
such commerce.

4

The mark is used by applying it to[5] _____

_____

and five specimens showing the mark as actually used are presented herewith.

6

_____ ,
 (name of partner)
being hereby warned that willful false statements and the like so made are punishable by fine or imprisonment, or both, under Section 1001 of Title 18 of the United States Code and that such willful false statements may jeopardize the validity of the application or any registration resulting therefrom, declares that he/she is a partner of applicant partnership; he/she believes said partnership to be the owner of the trademark sought to be registered; to the best of his/her knowledge and belief no other person, firm, corporation, or association has the right to use said mark in commerce, either in the identical form or in such near resemblance thereto as may be likely, when applied to the goods of such other person, to cause confusion, or to cause mistake, or to deceive; the facts set forth in this application are true; and all statements made of his/her own knowledge are true and all statements made on information and belief are believed to be true.

_____
 (signature of partner)

_____
 (date)

Form PTO - 1477 (4 - 82)   *(Instructions on reverse side)*   Patent and Trademark Office - U.S. DEPT. of COMMERCE
 (over)

TRADEMARK APPLICATION FORM.

REPRESENTATION

If the applicant is not domiciled in the United States, a domestic representative·must be designated. See Form 4.4.

If applicant wishes to furnish a power of attorney, see Form 4.2. An attorney at law is not required to furnish a power.

FOOTNOTES

1   If registration is sought for a word or numeral mark not depicted in any special form, the drawing may be the mark typed in capital letters on letter-size bond paper; otherwise, the drawing should be made with india ink on a good grade of bond paper or on bristol board.

2   If more than one item of goods in a class is set forth and the dates given for that class apply to only one of the items listed, insert the name of the item to which the dates apply.

3   Type of commerce should be specified as "interstate," "territorial," "foreign," or other type of commerce which may lawfully be regulated by Congress. Foreign applicants relying upon use must specify commerce which Congress may regulate, using wording such as commerce with the United States or commerce between the United States and a foreign country.

4   If the mark is other than a coined, arbitrary or fanciful mark, and the mark is believed to have acquired a secondary meaning, insert whichever of the following paragraphs is applicable:

   a) The mark has become distinctive of applicant's goods as a result of substantially exclusive and continuous

   use in _____ commerce for the five years next preceding the date of filing
                (type of commerce)
   of this application.

   b) The mark has become distinctive of applicant's goods as evidenced by the showing submitted separately.

5   Insert the manner or method of using the mark with the goods, i.e., "the goods," "the containers for the goods," "displays associated with the goods," "tags or labels affixed to the goods," or other method which may be in use.

6   The required fee of $175.00 for each class must be submitted. (An application to register the same mark for goods and/or services in more than one class may be filed; however, goods and/or services and dates of use, by class, must be set out separately, and specimens and a fee for each class are required.)

in a publication. In either situation, you would be barred from obtaining a patent.
5. Proceed with caution. Given the potentially high stakes involved, it's important to be informed each step of the way.

To get the basic facts on obtaining a patent, read "Patents and Inventions: An Information Aid for Inventors," published by the U.S. Department of Commerce, Patent and Trademark Office, Washington, D.C. 20231.

Copyrights

A copyright protects the right of an individual to keep others from copying his or her artistic creations. Although most commonly associated with literary works, copyright protection extends to paintings, graphic designs, sculpture, musical compositions, sound recordings, and audiovisual works. Included within this broad coverage are such diverse forms as catalogs and advertising copy, photographs, charts, technical drawings, and computer programs. Thus, whether or not your home-based business is directly involved in the arts, you may still be able to benefit from copyright protection.

Obtaining a copyright is considerably easier than getting a trademark or patent. Essentially, it involves providing public notice of the copyright ("Copyright © 1991, Seymour Ferris") and filing an application for it (see pages 36–37). At this writing, the fee for this is $20, and the registration process can usually be completed without the assistance of an attorney. Once granted, a copyright is valid for up to fifty years after the holder's death. To receive all the relevant information on copyrights, as well as the appropriate application form, write to the Copyright Office, Library of Congress, Washington, D.C. 20559. Be sure to specify the nature of the work to be copyrighted so that you will receive the correct form.

CHOOSING YOUR LEGAL STRUCTURE

Part of keeping your home-based business legal involves choosing the legal structure for it: sole proprietorship, partnership, or corporation. Aside from being necessary for government reporting and tax purposes, this can enable your business to operate more efficiently. Since each legal form has its own unique characteristics, your goal is to choose the form that works best for you.

Sole Proprietorship

A business owned by one person, who is entitled to all of its profits and responsible for all of its debts, is considered a sole proprietorship. Providing maximum control and minimum government interference, this legal form is currently used by more than 75 percent of all businesses. The main advantages that differentiate the sole proprietorship from the other legal forms are (1) the ease with which it can be started, (2) the owner's freedom to make decisions, and (3) the distribution of profits (owner takes all).

Still, the sole proprietorship isn't without disadvantages, the most serious of which is its unlimited liability. As a sole proprietor, you are responsible for all business debts. Should these exceed the assets of your business, your creditors can claim your personal assets—home, automobile, savings account, investments. Sole proprietorships also tend to have more difficulty obtaining capital and holding on to key employees. This stems from the fact that sole proprietorships generally have fewer resources and offer less opportunity for job advancement. Thus, anyone who chooses the sole proprietorship should be prepared to be a generalist, performing a variety of functions, from accounting to advertising.

Partnership

A business owned by two or more people, who agree to share in its profits, is considered a partnership. Like the

FORM TX
UNITED STATES COPYRIGHT OFFICE

REGISTRATION NUMBER

| TX | TXU |

EFFECTIVE DATE OF REGISTRATION

Month   Day   Year

DO NOT WRITE ABOVE THIS LINE. IF YOU NEED MORE SPACE, USE A SEPARATE CONTINUATION SHEET.

1

TITLE OF THIS WORK ▼

PREVIOUS OR ALTERNATIVE TITLES ▼

PUBLICATION AS A CONTRIBUTION   If this work was published as a contribution to a periodical, serial, or collection, give information about the collective work in which the contribution appeared.   **Title of Collective Work ▼**

If published in a periodical or serial give: **Volume ▼**   **Number ▼**   **Issue Date ▼**   **On Pages ▼**

2

a

NAME OF AUTHOR ▼

DATES OF BIRTH AND DEATH
Year Born ▼   Year Died ▼

Was this contribution to the work a "work made for hire"?
☐ Yes
☐ No

AUTHOR'S NATIONALITY OR DOMICILE
Name of Country
OR { Citizen of ▶_____
      Domiciled in ▶_____

WAS THIS AUTHOR'S CONTRIBUTION TO THE WORK
Anonymous?   ☐ Yes ☐ No
Pseudonymous?   ☐ Yes ☐ No

If the answer to either of these questions is "Yes," see detailed instructions

NATURE OF AUTHORSHIP   Briefly describe nature of the material created by this author in which copyright is claimed. ▼

NOTE
Under the law, the "author" of a "work made for hire" is generally the employer, not the employee (see instructions). For any part of this work that was "made for hire" check "Yes" in the space provided, give the employer (or other person for whom the work was prepared) as "Author" of that part, and leave the space for dates of birth and death blank.

b

NAME OF AUTHOR ▼

DATES OF BIRTH AND DEATH
Year Born ▼   Year Died ▼

Was this contribution to the work a "work made for hire"?
☐ Yes
☐ No

AUTHOR'S NATIONALITY OR DOMICILE
Name of country
OR { Citizen of ▶_____
      Domiciled in ▶_____

WAS THIS AUTHOR'S CONTRIBUTION TO THE WORK
Anonymous?   ☐ Yes ☐ No
Pseudonymous?   ☐ Yes ☐ No

If the answer to either of these questions is "Yes," see detailed instructions

NATURE OF AUTHORSHIP   Briefly describe nature of the material created by this author in which copyright is claimed. ▼

c

NAME OF AUTHOR ▼

DATES OF BIRTH AND DEATH
Year Born ▼   Year Died ▼

Was this contribution to the work a "work made for hire"?
☐ Yes
☐ No

AUTHOR'S NATIONALITY OR DOMICILE
Name of Country
OR { Citizen of ▶_____
      Domiciled in ▶_____

WAS THIS AUTHOR'S CONTRIBUTION TO THE WORK
Anonymous?   ☐ Yes ☐ No
Pseudonymous?   ☐ Yes ☐ No

If the answer to either of these questions is "Yes," see detailed instructions

NATURE OF AUTHORSHIP   Briefly describe nature of the material created by this author in which copyright is claimed. ▼

3

YEAR IN WHICH CREATION OF THIS WORK WAS COMPLETED This information must be given in all cases.   ◄ Year

DATE AND NATION OF FIRST PUBLICATION OF THIS PARTICULAR WORK
Complete this information ONLY if this work has been published.   Month ▶_____   Day ▶_____   Year ▶_____   ◄ Nation

4

See instructions before completing this space.

COPYRIGHT CLAIMANT(S) Name and address must be given even if the claimant is the same as the author given in space 2.▼

TRANSFER If the claimant(s) named here in space 4 are different from the author(s) named in space 2, give a brief statement of how the claimant(s) obtained ownership of the copyright.▼

APPLICATION RECEIVED

ONE DEPOSIT RECEIVED

TWO DEPOSITS RECEIVED

REMITTANCE NUMBER AND DATE

DO NOT WRITE HERE OFFICE USE ONLY

MORE ON BACK ▶   • Complete all applicable spaces (numbers 5-11) on the reverse side of this page.
• See detailed instructions.   • Sign the form at line 10.

DO NOT WRITE HERE
Page 1 of_____pages

COPYRIGHT APPLICATION FORM.

EXAMINED BY	FORM TX
CHECKED BY	

☐ CORRESPONDENCE Yes

☐ DEPOSIT ACCOUNT FUNDS USED

FOR
COPYRIGHT
OFFICE
USE
ONLY

DO NOT WRITE ABOVE THIS LINE. IF YOU NEED MORE SPACE, USE A SEPARATE CONTINUATION SHEET.

PREVIOUS REGISTRATION Has registration for this work, or for an earlier version of this work, already been made in the Copyright Office?
☐ Yes ☐ No If your answer is "Yes," why is another registration being sought? (Check appropriate box) ▼
☐ This is the first published edition of a work previously registered in unpublished form.
☐ This is the first application submitted by this author as copyright claimant.
☐ This is a changed version of the work, as shown by space 6 on this application.
If your answer is "Yes," give: **Previous Registration Number ▼**   **Year of Registration ▼**

5

DERIVATIVE WORK OR COMPILATION Complete both space 6a & 6b for a derivative work; complete only 6b for a compilation.
a. Preexisting Material Identify any preexisting work or works that this work is based on or incorporates. ▼

b. Material Added to This Work Give a brief, general statement of the material that has been added to this work and in which copyright is claimed. ▼

6

See instructions
before completing
this space.

MANUFACTURERS AND LOCATIONS If this is a published work consisting preponderantly of nondramatic literary material in English, the law may require that the copies be manufactured in the United States or Canada for full protection. If so, the names of the manufacturers who performed certain processes, and the places where these processes were performed must be given. See instructions for details.
Names of Manufacturers ▼   **Places of Manufacture ▼**

7

REPRODUCTION FOR USE OF BLIND OR PHYSICALLY HANDICAPPED INDIVIDUALS   A signature on this form at space 10, and a check in one of the boxes here in space 8, constitutes a non-exclusive grant of permission to the Library of Congress to reproduce and distribute solely for the blind and physically handicapped and under the conditions and limitations prescribed by the regulations of the Copyright Office: (1) copies of the work identified in space 1 of this application in Braille (or similar tactile symbols); or (2) phonorecords embodying a fixation of a reading of that work; or (3) both.
a ☐ Copies and Phonorecords   b ☐ Copies Only   c ☐ Phonorecords Only

8

See instructions.

DEPOSIT ACCOUNT If the registration fee is to be charged to a Deposit Account established in the Copyright Office, give name and number of Account.
Name ▼   **Account Number ▼**

9

CORRESPONDENCE Give name and address to which correspondence about this application should be sent. Name/Address/Apt/City/State/Zip ▼

Area Code & Telephone Number ▶

Be sure to
give your
daytime phone
◀ number

CERTIFICATION* I, the undersigned, hereby certify that I am the

Check one ▶

☐ author
☐ other copyright claimant
☐ owner of exclusive right(s)
☐ authorized agent of _____

of the work identified in this application and that the statements made
by me in this application are correct to the best of my knowledge.

Name of author or other copyright claimant, or owner of exclusive right(s) ▲

10

Typed or printed name and date ▼ If this is a published work, this date must be the same as or later than the date of publication given in space 3.

_____ date ▶ _____

Handwritten signature (X) ▼

MAIL CERTIFI-CATE TO

Name ▼

Number/Street/Apartment Number ▼

City/State/ZIP ▼

Certificate will be mailed in window envelope

Have you:
• Completed all necessary spaces?
• Signed your application in space 10?
• Enclosed check or money order for $10 payable to *Register of Copyrights*?
• Enclosed your deposit material with the application and fee?
MAIL TO: Register of Copyrights, Library of Congress, Washington, D.C. 20559

11

* 17 U.S.C. § 506(e): Any person who knowingly makes a false representation of a material fact in the application for copyright registration provided for by section 409, or in any written statement filed in connection with the application, shall be fined not more than $2,500.

☆ U.S. GOVERNMENT PRINTING OFFICE: 1982-361-278/58

Sept. 1982—600,000

sole proprietorship, it is easy to start and the red tape involved is usually minimal. The main advantages of the partnership form are that the business can (1) draw on the skills and abilities of each partner, (2) offer employees the opportunity to become partners, and (3) utilize the partners' combined financial resources. However, for your own protection, it's advisable to have a written partnership agreement. This should state (1) each partner's rights and responsibilities, (2) the amount of capital each partner is investing in the business, (3) the distribution of profits, (4) what happens if a partner joins or leaves the business, and (5) how the assets are to be divided if the business is discontinued.

Partnerships also have their share of disadvantages. The unlimited liability that applies to sole proprietorships is even worse for partnerships. As a partner, you are responsible not only for your own business debts, but for those of your partners as well. Should they incur debts or legal judgments against the business, you could be held legally responsible for them. Disputes among partners can be a problem, too. Unless you and your partners see eye to eye on how the business should be run and what it should accomplish, you're in for trouble.

Corporation

A corporation differs from the other legal forms of business in that the law regards it as an artificial being possessing the same rights and responsibilities as a person. This means that, unlike sole proprietorships or partnerships, it has an existence separate from its owners. As a result, the corporation offers some unique advantages. These include (1) limited liability: owners are not personally responsible for the debts of the business, (2) the ability to raise capital by selling shares of stock, and (3) easy transfer of ownership from one individual to another. Plus, unlike the sole proprietorship and partnership, the corporation has "unlimited life" and thus the potential to outlive its original owners.

The main disadvantage of the corporate form can be

THE ADVANTAGES AND DISADVANTAGES OF EACH LEGAL FORM OF OWNERSHIP

Sole Proprietorship

Advantages	Disadvantages
1. You're the boss.	1. You assume unlimited liability.
2. It's easy to get started.	
3. You keep all profits.	2. The amount of investment capital you can raise is limited.
4. Income from business is taxed as personal income.	3. You need to be a generalist.
5. You can discontinue your business at will.	4. Retaining high-caliber employees is difficult.
	5. The life of the business is limited.

Partnership

Advantages	Disadvantages
1. Two heads are better than one.	1. Partners have unlimited liability.
2. It's easy to get started.	2. Partners must share all profits.
3. More investment capital is available.	3. The partners may disagree.
4. Partners pay only personal income tax.	4. The life of the business is limited.
5. High-caliber employees can be made partners.	

Corporation

Advantages	Disadvantages
1. Stockholders have limited liability.	1. Corporations are taxed twice.
2. Corporations can raise the most investment capital.	2. Corporations must pay capital stock tax.
3. Corporations have unlimited life.	3. Starting a corporation is expensive.
4. Ownership is easily transferable.	4. Corporations are closely regulated by government agencies.
5. Corporations utilize specialists.	

summed up in two words: *taxation* and *complexity*. In what amounts to double taxation, you must pay taxes on both the income the corporation earns and the income you earn as an individual. Along with this, corporations are required to pay an annual tax on all outstanding shares of stock. Given its complexity, a corporation is both more difficult and more expensive to start than are the sole proprietorship and the partnership. In order to form a corporation, you must be granted a charter by the state in which your home-based business is located. For a small business the cost of incorporating usually ranges from $500 to $1,500. This includes the costs for legal assistance in drawing up your charter, state incorporation fees, and the purchase of record books and stock certificates. And, since corporations are subject to closer regulation by the government, the owners must bear the ongoing cost of preparing and filing state and federal reports.

S Corporation

If you are interested in forming a corporation, but hesitate to do so because of the double taxation, there is a way to avoid it. You can do this by making your business an S corporation. The Internal Revenue Service permits this type of corporation to be taxed as a partnership rather than a corporation. However, in order to qualify for S status, your business must meet the specific requirements set forth by the IRS. These include limits on (1) the number and type of shareholders in the business, (2) the stock that is issued, (3) the corporation's sources of revenues. For more information on forming an S corporation, ask the IRS for its free publication, *Tax Guide for Small Business*, publication number 334.

TIPS ON KEEPING YOUR BUSINESS LEGAL

1. Before you start your home-based business, find out what government regulations specifically apply to your type of business.

2. Check with the weekly newspapers in your area to get the lowest rate for publishing your fictitious business name statement.
3. If you plan to operate your business under more than one fictitious name, you can save on filing fees by listing all names on one statement (up to five names are allowed).
4. When applying for a seller's permit, remember that the lower your estimated sales for the year, the less money you will have to post as a bond.
5. Keep a copy of your seller's permit in your wallet or purse so that it's always handy when you need it.
6. Reduce your overhead and paperwork by utilizing subcontractors instead of employees whenever feasible.
7. If your business is a partnership, be sure to obtain an IRS employer identification number whether you have employees or not. This is required for your tax return.
8. Weigh the advantages and disadvantages of each legal form before selecting the one to use for your business.
9. If you are unable to patent your invention, you may still be able to use a trademark or copyright to protect your rights to it.
10. Utilize the services of attorneys or other experts in complying with government regulations, structuring your business, or obtaining a patent or trademark.

4

Convincing Lenders to Say Yes

AT the same time you are establishing your home-based business, you should also be establishing a good credit rating. Whether or not you need to borrow money in the beginning, it's likely that you will need to eventually as your business grows. For example, you might need capital to replace outdated equipment, purchase supplies and merchandise, remodel or expand your work area, or deal with an emergency. In any event, the greater your ability to convince lenders that you can repay their money on time and with the appropriate interest, the greater your borrowing power will be.

ESTABLISHING A GOOD CREDIT RATING

The best way to establish a good credit rating is to demonstrate your ability to manage the credit you already have. This means paying department store, gasoline, and bank charge accounts on time; sticking to rent-, mortgage-, and automobile-payment schedules; and honoring all other debts. As a home-based entrepreneur, you must also watch your expenses and operate your business according to the acceptable practices for your industry.

The Importance of Doing Your Homework

As the degree of risk associated with lending you money goes down, the probability of getting your loan approved goes up. One way to lower the risk is to anticipate the kinds of questions lenders will ask you. For example, prior to filling out a loan application, you should know (1) exactly how much money you need, (2) how you plan to use the money, (3) how long it will take you to repay the loan, (4) what rate of interest you can afford, and (5) what you can use as security for the loan. Surprisingly, many loan applicants don't have the faintest idea how or when they intend to repay the money they have requested. Often they don't even know how much money they need. When asked how much money they want to borrow, many people give these two common responses: "How much money can I get?" and "As much as possible." Is it any wonder that lenders say no? The bottom line is that it pays to do your homework *before* you ask for a loan.

Part of that homework is to gather the financial data that will enable you to prove to lenders that you are a good credit risk. In short, this entails putting together a credit history that includes the following:

- A list of all credit cards and their current balances
- All outstanding loans, including original balances, amounts outstanding, and current monthly payments
- Total monthly mortgage or rent payments
- Net monthly income from your home-based business, an outside job, or other sources
- Checking and savings account balances
- The value of your automobile(s), including original cost, balance owed, and current monthly payments
- The current value of all property, including real estate, stocks, and bonds

It's also important to have a *written business plan* explaining in detail your business objectives, projected earnings for the next one to three years, marketing strategy, and other relevant information.

The Six C's of Credit

Armed with this information, you're now ready to approach lenders. In so doing, though, you should be aware of the criteria against which your loan application will be evaluated. Known as the *six C's of credit*, these are: capital, collateral, capability, character, coverage, and circumstances.

In lending terminology, the amount of *capital* you have is the amount of money you have invested in your business or have available for future investment. Your *collateral* consists of the specific assets, if any, that you could pledge as security for the loan. Your *capability* (to repay the loan) is measured in terms of your monthly income and current level of debt. *Character*, albeit harder to evaluate, is determined on the basis of your reputation and credit history. Any insurance or safety precautions that may be necessary to protect the lender's investment come under the heading of *coverage*. And the *circumstances* include both your individual financial situation and the state of the economy in general.

The importance that lenders place on each of these six C's of credit depends on the type of loan you are seeking. In the case of an equipment loan, for instance, the equipment itself becomes the collateral. As such, one of the lender's main concerns is coverage. To protect itself in the event that the equipment is damaged or stolen, the lender would require you to obtain adequate insurance. The remaining C's, though still relevant, have less bearing on such a loan since it is secured by collateral and insurance. In granting an unsecured loan, however, such as one to provide working capital to meet everyday business expenses, lenders will look at other details. In loans of this type, the greatest weight is likely to be placed on your capability and character.

TYPES OF LENDERS

It isn't just the loans that differ, but the lenders themselves—both the individuals and the institutions. What's acceptable to one lender may not be to another. A loan that's rejected outright by one lending institution may be approved as a matter of course by a second. What's more, the interest rates charged by lenders can vary as well. At first, this lack of standardized practices may seem confusing or even unfair. But it can also be viewed as an opportunity. Instead of being forced to conform to one set of loan standards, the prospective borrower has a variety of financing options from which to choose. And, as with any other major purchase, it's a good idea to shop and compare before you buy.

Commercial Banks

Commercial banks have traditionally been a major source of capital for both new and established businesses. Despite what you may have heard to the contrary, loan money *is* available. However, individual bank policies on how that money is to be distributed can vary widely. Some banks virtually restrict themselves to business loans whereas others specialize in consumer loans. Needless to say, this has a direct bearing on the acceptance or rejection of your loan application. The lesson to be learned from this is that if one bank turns you down, you should try another.

Because they want to remain competitive, banks do not all charge the same interest rates, either. A difference of 2 to 3 percent in interest rates is not uncommon. Although this might seem like a small amount, over the life of the loan it adds up. On a five-year loan for $25,000, for example, the difference between an interest rate of 14 percent and one of 17 percent totals almost $2,500. So, when shopping for a bank loan, take a close look at the interest rate you will be paying for it.

Savings and Loans

Savings and loan establishments most commonly give loans for home financing and improvement. Lately, though, many savings and loan companies have started to make business loans as well. Business loans must normally be repaid over a shorter period of time than home loans, thus enabling savings and loan companies to recoup their money faster. Taking this into consideration, you may want to do some research to see which savings and loan companies in your community grant business loans.

If you are a homeowner, you have another alternative. It may be possible for you to obtain indirect financing for your business by taking out a first or second mortgage on your home. In this instance, though, since the loan is made to you as an individual, rather than to your business, the interest payable on the loan cannot be deducted as a legitimate business expense. What's more, mortgaging your home can be risky, since a business loss could put your home in jeopardy.

Credit Unions

Credit unions generally offer lower interest rates than do banks or savings and loan institutions. But, in order to apply for a loan, you must be a member of the credit union. If you aren't already a member, you might want to explore the possibility of joining one. Established for the purpose of providing members with low-interest loans, credit unions are usually formed around an employer, professional organization, church, or fraternal group.

The types of loans most commonly made by credit unions are short-term consumer loans for automobiles, boats, furniture, and so on. However, you may be able to stretch the bounds of this category to encompass furnishings for your home-based business, equipment, or a company car. And, since computers are now considered "home furnishings," most credit unions will lend up to $5,000 for the purchase of a computer. In addition to this, if you have a good credit rating, you might qualify for a personal signature loan up to $10,000. Such a loan is granted on the basis of your capacity and character alone and requires no collateral.

Small Business Administration

The Small Business Administration (SBA) is a federal agency created in 1953 for the purpose of providing businesses with both advice and financial aid. Its interest rates are the same as or lower than those of banks and savings and loan associations, but it allows longer repayment periods. By law, though, the SBA is not permitted to compete with other lenders. Calling itself the "lender of last resort," the SBA's usual practice is to work in partnership with lending institutions, guaranteeing small business loans for up to 90 percent of the loan amount. In some instances, however, the SBA will make direct loans to entrepreneurs who cannot obtain debt financing from any other source.

In granting loans, the SBA tends to favor businesses that provide a family's primary source of income. Thus, if your home-based business is a full-time operation rather than a sideline business, you have a better chance of obtaining SBA financing. It also helps if you can show that you have already invested your own money in the business. Generally the SBA wants at least 20 percent of the start-up capital to come from you. Along with these financial considerations, the SBA evaluates the business itself and the loan applicant to determine if he or she has the experience and character to make the business a success. The Personal Financial Statement shown on pages 48–49 should give you an idea of the kind of information the SBA and other lenders expect to see. For more information on SBA loans, look in the White Pages of your telephone directory under "United States Government, Small Business Administration" to locate the SBA field office closest to you. Or you can write to the Small Business Administration, Washington, D.C. 20417.

Small Business Investment Companies

Small Business Investment Companies (SBICs) are privately owned and operated companies that provide long-term financing to businesses. The formation of these com-

	OMB Approval No. 3245-0188 Exp. Date: 10-31-89

PERSONAL FINANCIAL STATEMENT

As of _____ 19 ____

Complete this form if 1) a sole proprietorship by the proprietor; 2) a partnership by each partner; 3) a corporation by each officer and each stockholder with 20% or more ownership; 4) any other person or entity providing a guaranty on the loan.

Name _____ Residence Phone _____

Residence Address _____

City, State, & Zip _____

Business Name of Applicant/Borrower _____

ASSETS	(Omit Cents)	LIABILITIES	(Omit Cents)
Cash on hand & in Banks.................	$_____	Accounts Payable	$_____
Savings Accounts.........................	_____	Notes Payable (to Bk & Others	
IRA	_____	(Describe in Section 2)...............	_____
Accounts & Notes Receivable		Installment Account (Auto)	
(Describe in Section 6)	_____	Mo. Payments $_____	_____
Life Insurance—Cash		Installment Account (Other)	
Surrender Value Only	_____	Mo. Payments $_____	_____
Stocks and Bonds		Loans on Life Insurance	_____
(Describe in Section 3)	_____	Mortgages on Real Estate.............	_____
Real Estate		(Describe in Section 4)...............	_____
(Describe in Section 4)	_____	Unpaid Taxes	
Automobile—Present Value	_____	(Describe in Section 7)...............	_____
Other Personal Property	_____	Other Liabilities	
(Describe in Section 5)	_____	(Describe in Section 8)...............	_____
Other Assets			
(Describe in Section 6)	_____	Total Liabilities......................	_____
		Net Worth	_____
Total.................	$_____	Total......................	$_____

Section 1. Source of Income		Contingent Liabilities	
Salary	$_____	As Endorser or Co-Maker	$_____
Net Investment Income	_____	Legal Claims & Judgments	_____
Real Estate Income	_____	Provision for Fed Income Tax......................	_____
Other Income (Describe)*	_____	Other Special Debt	_____

Description of Items Listed in Section I _____

*(Alimony or child support payments need not be disclosed in "Other Income" unless it is desired to have such payments counted toward total income.)

Section 2. Notes Payable to Banks and Others

Name & Address of Noteholder	Original Balance	Current Balance	Payment Amount	Terms (Monthly-etc.)	How Secured or Endorsed—Type of Collateral

SBA Form 413 (10-87)   Use 10-86 edition until exhausted   Refer to SOP 50   10

(Response is required to obtain a benefit)

A PERSONAL FINANCIAL STATEMENT

Section 3. Stocks and Bonds: (*Use separate sheet if necessary*)

No. of Shares	Names of Securities	Cost	Market Value Quotation/Exchange	Date Amount

Section 4. Real Estate Owned. (*List each parcel separately. Use supplemental sheets if necessary. Each sheet must be identified as a supplement to this statement and signed*).

Address—Type of property	Title is in name of	Date Purchased	Original Cost	Present Value	Mortgage Balance	Amount of Payment	Status of Mortgage

Section 5. Other Personal Property. (*Describe, and if any is mortgaged, state name and address of mortgage holder and amount of mortgage, terms of payment, and if delinquent, describe delinquency.*)

Section 6. Other Assets, Notes & Accounts Receivable (Describe)

Section 7. Unpaid Taxes. (*Describe in detail, as to type, to whom payable, when due, amount, and what, if any, property the tax lien attaches*)

Section 8. Other Liabilities. (*Describe in detail*)

Section 9. Life Insurance Held (*Give face amount of policies—name of company and beneficiaries*)

SBA/Lender is authorized to make all inquiries deemed necessary to verify the accuracy of the statements made herein and to determine my/our creditworthiness.
(I) or (We) certify the above and the statements contained in the schedules herein are a true and accurate statement of (my) or (our) financial condition as of the date stated herein. This statement is given for the purpose of: (*Check one of the following*)

☐ Inducing S.B.A. to grant a loan as requested in the application, to the individual or firm whose name appears herein.
☐ Furnishing a statement of (my) or (our) financial condition, pursuant to the terms of the guaranty executed by (me) or (us) at the same time S.B.A. granted a loan to the individual or firm, whose name appears herein.

Signature	Signature	Date

SOCIAL SECURITY NO.	SOCIAL SECURITY NO.

SBA Form 413 (10-87)

panies was authorized by the Small Business Investment Act of 1958. In accordance with this act, SBICs are licensed (and frequently financed) by the Small Business Administration. As such, they are required to conform to SBA regulations. Aside from that, however, each SBIC is different; each has its own policies and preferences when it comes to business financing. For example, some SBICs are primarily lenders whereas others are actually investors seeking part ownership in the businesses they finance. Along with this, many SBICs specialize in providing assistance to certain industries such as high technology, retailing, film production, and so on. If you would like to know more about Small Business Investment Companies, contact your local SBA field office.

Life Insurance Companies

Life insurance companies are a source of business financing that often goes unnoticed. Yet, as a result of the premiums they collect, these companies frequently have large reserves of cash available for investment purposes. Aside from making direct loans to businesses, life insurance companies will allow individuals to borrow against their insurance policies provided that those policies have cash value. Policies that don't build up cash value (term insurance for example), and those with insufficient amounts of money paid into them are not acceptable as collateral. Since a loan of this type is essentially a loan from yourself, there are no restrictions on how you can use the money, be it to take a vacation or invest in your business. Furthermore, when you borrow against your insurance policy, the interest rates are usually much lower than those charged by other lenders.

Finance Companies

Finance companies do business by making loans that banks and other lenders regard as too risky. They make both secured and unsecured loans, and they lend money for virtually any purpose. Known for their liberal credit policies and speedy loan processing, finance companies pro-

FEDERAL ENFORCEMENT AGENCIES

Consumer Credit Protection

Credit Unions

Division of Consumer Affairs
National Credit Union Administration
Washington, D.C. 20456

Finance Companies, Debt Collectors, Credit Reporting Agencies, and Department Stores

Division of Credit Practices
Federal Trade Commission
Washington, D.C. 20580

National Banks

Comptroller of the Currency
Department of the Treasury
Washington, D.C. 20219

Nonmember Insured Banks

Office of Consumer Affairs and Civil Rights
Federal Deposit Insurance Corporation
Washington, D.C. 20429

Savings and Loan Associations

Consumer Division, Office of
Community Investment
Federal Home Loan Bank Board
Washington, D.C. 20552

Small Business Investment Companies

Small Business Administration
Washington, D.C. 20416

State Member Banks

Division of Consumer Affairs
Board of Governments of the Federal Reserve
  System
Washington, D.C. 20551

vide borrowers with another financing alternative—but an expensive one. Proof that convenience comes at a price is the considerably higher interest rates that finance companies charge. Keeping this in mind, your focus may shift from getting the finance company to say yes to determining whether or not to accept its offer. Other options include: requesting a smaller amount, postponing the loan until you can obtain more favorable financing, or forgoing the loan altogether.

GETTING TO KNOW YOUR BANKER

As a home-based businessperson, you should also make it a point to get to know your banker. He or she can be a valuable business ally, providing a variety of financial information, advice, and services. These include helping you to bill customers, prepare financial reports, obtain a line of credit, make purchasing decisions, invest your money, transfer funds, and so on. Furthermore, since bankers come into contact with different segments of the community, your banker may be in a position to hear news that affects your business before you do.

The time to begin developing a good working relationship with your banker is when your business is still in the planning stage. Your first move should be to open a checking account in the name of your business. Aside from making it easier for you to pay and keep track of business-related expenses, this signals others that you are serious about developing your home-based business into a viable enterprise. What's more, opening a checking account gives you a perfect opportunity to introduce yourself to the manager of the bank branch where your banking transactions will take place.

At your first meeting with the bank manager, your goal is simply to open a channel of communication between the two of you. Rather than just being another number on a ledger, you want to differentiate your account from the others. Here a brief summary of your background and business objectives can add another dimension to the facts already on paper. The entire meeting might last only a few minutes, but if it lays the groundwork for future communication, it will have served its purpose. Toward this end, you might offer to keep the banker posted on the progress of your business by sending your financial reports to the bank on a regular basis. Then, in the event that you need advice or wish to apply for a loan at a later date, the banker will already know something about you.

CREDIT WHERE CREDIT IS DUE

As a rule of thumb, if you use credit well, you should have little difficulty in getting more of it. For good measure, though, it helps to be aware of federal consumer credit laws and the ways in which they affect your right to credit. The most far-reaching of these credit laws stem from three acts:

- *Equal Credit Opportunity Act*—prohibits creditors from denying credit on the basis of age, sex, marital status, race, color, national origin, or religion.
- *Fair Credit Reporting Act*—protects consumers against the circulation of inaccurate or obsolete credit information.
- *Truth in Lending Act*—requires creditors to reveal specific information about the cost of buying credit or taking out a loan.

Together these acts set the basic standards for how consumers are to be treated in their credit dealings. Along with this, the acts stipulate that creditors who fail to comply with the law can be sued for damages. Take the Equal Credit Opportunity Act, for example: If you believe that a creditor has discriminated against you in some way, you may sue for damages up to $10,000 plus court and attorney's fees.

The chart on page 51 shows the federal enforcement agencies to contact if you wish to bring a complaint against a creditor.

TIPS ON HOW TO GET A LOAN

1. Open a separate checking account in the name of your business.
2. Get to know your banker by name and establish a good working relationship.
3. Try to anticipate and prepare for the kinds of questions lenders will ask.
4. Gather your financial data in advance so that it is ready to be presented to lenders.
5. Be candid about any credit problems you may have had in the past; these are likely to show up in a routine credit check, anyway.
6. Don't ask for more credit than you can realistically repay.
7. Know how your business's financial status compares with that of other similar businesses.
8. Compare the various financing options available to determine which one offers the most favorable terms.
9. Don't get discouraged if your loan isn't approved by the first lender you contact; persistence pays.
10. After you receive a loan, be sure to keep the lender informed about new developments in your business.

5

Furnishing Your Business

FURNISHING your home-based business doesn't have to be an elaborate or costly production. Through careful planning you can create a work environment that is both attractive and efficient—and still stay within your budget. The ingenuity you bring to the project is more important than the amount of money you have to spend, or the amount of space available for your business.

MAXIMIZING SPACE

One thing all home-based businesspersons have in common is the need to make the most efficient use of whatever space is available. Whether your business uses the latest in computer equipment or a turn-of-the-century hand loom, you will probably wish you had more available space in which to operate. More often than not, though, lack of space isn't the real problem. Rather, it's poor utilization of the existing space.

Discovering Hidden Space

Even the smallest apartment has space that is ignored or underutilized. But, because people tend to see their en-

vironments in just one way—the way they already are—
this space, for all practical purposes, remains hidden, in
spite of the fact that the space may be in plain view and
easily accessible.

Tapping the hidden space in your home to provide the
maximum amount for your business means putting aside
set ideas about how a room or area should be used. What's
needed here isn't so much a knowledge of interior design
as a willingness to be flexible. For instance, what rule states
that a bed always has to be in the bedroom? Or, for that
matter, that a bed always has to remain in the same place
day and night? If space is at a premium, a convertible sofabed
or a Murphy bed can free the space that would otherwise
be taken up by a conventional bed. Some home-based entrepreneurs have even gone one step further by putting their
beds on platforms high off the floor, thereby creating work
areas in the space underneath. This isn't as farfetched as it
might seem. In fact, a number of combination bed-desk-
storage units currently on the market were designed ex-
pressly for the purpose of creating a work space.

Other examples of hidden space that often can be used
for home-based businesses include closets, alcoves, window
seats, attics, basements, pantries, garages, and even the
space underneath stairways. By replacing clothing rods
with inexpensive shelving, you can convert a standard
closet into a storage area for supplies and merchandise.
Or you may want to fit a desk or computer equipment into
the space instead. The typical garage—jam-packed with
old toys, clothing, furniture, newspapers, and other
discards—is another space that could be an ideal location
for a home-based business. In most cases extensive remodeling isn't needed, just a coat of paint, appropriate
lighting, and possibly do-it-yourself flooring to cover the
foundation.

Multipurpose Space

Barring the possibility of discovering a space that can be
devoted exclusively to your business, there is still another

alternative open to you: using multipurpose, or shared, space. To capitalize on this, though, you will have to do some rethinking about how each room or area in your home is currently being used. Instead of assuming that the living room is solely for entertaining, the dining room solely for eating, and so on, you must be willing to consider other uses for these spaces. With the proper furnishings a space that currently serves just one purpose can become a multipurpose area. Installing a partition or room divider to create two spaces in one, adding storage cabinets, or simply using furniture and accessories that are collapsible or portable will enable practically any space to double as a home business.

For inspiration, or ideas on how to maximize space, one has only to look at the Japanese culture. The Japanese have taken the concept of multipurpose space and raised it to an art form. By folding, stacking, and carrying the household articles they use each day, they make these items fit into small areas. Japanese beds, called *futons*, are folded and stored in cabinets when not in use. Dishes, serving trays, and tables are stacked on top of one another. Home furnishings are light and portable so that they can be easily carried from one room to another as the need arises. In this way one room can be made to serve the purpose of three (or even more) rooms, being used in turn as a bedroom, dining room, and living room.

INCREASING EFFICIENCY

Fitting your home-based business into its surroundings is only half the battle. What remains to be done is to set it up in a way that will enable you to operate at peak efficiency. In a word, this means having a suitable layout.

Layout

A well-designed layout not only maximizes space but increases efficiency as well. The basic rule of interior design is that form should follow function. Applied to your home-based business, this means that the various functions you perform—creating, selling, shipping, storing, managing— should determine the arrangement of furniture, equipment, supplies, and merchandise. You can eliminate the need to run back and forth between the telephone and the filing cabinet, your work area and the supply area, by moving them as close together as possible. Keeping within reach those things you most often use saves steps and allows you to be more productive.

Maintenance

Another way to increase efficiency is to reduce maintenance to the bare minimum. Choosing furniture made out of soil-resistant materials means you'll spend less time cleaning it. By the same token, floor and wall coverings should be durable and easily washable. This is all the more important if your home-based business is a studio or workshop, since considerable wear and tear on furnishings can be expected. As for equipment—such as an electric typewriter, computer, word processor, or duplicating machine —be sure to find out what kind of maintenance it needs before you buy or lease it. You will save time and money by choosing equipment that is easy and economical to maintain.

Comfort Level

Determining what your comfort level is can go a long way toward increasing your efficiency, too. The term "comfort level" refers to the environmental conditions—light, heat, ventilation—that are most comfortable for you. A poorly illuminated desk, work table, or easel is not only uncomfortable to work at, but inefficient as well. The same holds true for a room that is too hot or too cold. And adequate ventilation is a must, especially if you're working with materials such as paint, wood stain, or glue that give off unpleasant odors.

CREATING THE PROPER IMAGE

Before purchasing any furniture or accessories for your home-based business, you should decide on the kind of image that you want to create. In addition to the overall look of your business, this also encompasses the way people feel about it. For example, do you want your environment to look and feel like a branch office of IBM? More along the lines of Santa's workshop? Or some point in between? In the first case, you are likely to be drawn to furnishings that are high-tech, modern, clean, and functional. The second case calls for furnishings of a different sort: whimsical, old-fashioned, warm, and comfortable.

Once you've decided on the appropriate image for your business, you must go about creating it. That task will rest largely on a combination of three elements: furniture, color, and lighting.

Furniture

The furniture you choose for your business says a great deal about you, whether you realize it or not. Even something as simple and basic as a desk can send a message to others, telling them about your personality, the quality of your products and services, and more. Two desks of equal value—one constructed out of chrome and glass, the other made of dark mahogany—present very different images. The first conveys a futuristic feeling and says that the owner is unconventional and an original thinker. The second evokes a feeling of permanence and says that the owner is traditional and conservative. The other pieces of furniture that surround each desk can reinforce or modify these impressions. Thus, to put people at ease, you might soften the starkness of the chrome and glass desk by placing a comfortable sofa nearby where informal conversations can take place.

The thing to remember in selecting furniture, or rearranging existing furniture, is that each piece should be evaluated on the basis of what it can contribute to your total look. What counts isn't how much furniture your home-based business has, or even how expensive it is, but how appropriate it is for your needs. More information on this, along with suggestions for choosing furniture that works, is provided later in the chapter.

Color

Color also plays an important part in creating and maintaining an image. Research has shown that specific colors tend to affect people in similar ways. Blue, for example, has a soothing influence. Red stimulates the senses and generates a feeling of excitement. Yellow is an upbeat, cheery color. Brown is comfortable and reassuring. Neutral colors like beige and gray are restful.

Taking into consideration your own preferences and the effect you want to have on others, you can use color to bolster your image. For instance, a marriage counselor might choose colors that are relaxing and nonthreatening such as blue, green, and earth tones. The owner of an advertising agency would probably be better served by red, orange, and yellow, colors associated with a high degree of energy and creativity. Although people are more inclined to have positive color associations than negative ones, using the wrong color in a particular setting can also trigger a negative association. For example, white used in connection with food service generally has a positive association of cleanliness. However, an employment agency using white runs the risk of being perceived as sterile and impersonal.

To compare the emotional impact of colors and determine which ones would work best for you, refer to the Color Association Chart shown on page 61.

Lighting

Proper lighting serves the dual purpose of enhancing the appearance of your business and enabling you to be more productive. Without proper lighting you will find it diffi-

COLOR ASSOCIATION CHART

Color	Positive Associations	Negative Associations
Yellow	Cheerful, happy, upbeat, energetic, creative	Harsh, gaudy, overpowering
Gold	Tasteful, rich, ornate	Extravagant, wasteful
Brown	Sensible, reliable, consistent, trustworthy	Dull, ordinary, unoriginal
Orange	Outgoing, warm, affectionate, unconventional	Brash, pushy, gauche
Red	Extroverted, forceful, daring, passionate, exciting	Hot, violent, combative, temperamental
Pink	Soft, innocent, romantic	Frivolous, unsubstantial, immature
Purple	Sophisticated, majestic, intellectual	Snobbish, affected, superior
Blue	Soothing, peaceful, subdued, secure	Cold, wet, sad
Turquoise	Elegant, controlled, artistic	Haughty, smug, pretentious
Green	Restful, serene, cool	Moldy, slimy, medicinal
Silver	Traditional, established, sleek	Artificial, unrealistic, spendthrift
Gray	Refined, cultured, discriminating	Restrained, noncommittal, aloof
Black	Powerful, decisive	Aggressive, somber, deathlike
White	Clean, modern, fresh	Sterile, impersonal, stark

cult to display merchandise attractively, conduct meetings comfortably, or work efficiently. A vital element in creating an image, lighting can be used to make an area seem larger or smaller, warmer or cooler. It can establish a mood and direct one's attention to a particular spot. And, by improving visibility, it reduces eye strain, relieves tension, and helps prevent accidents.

If your home-based business occupies a room that is also used for nonbusiness activities (such as the living room or your bedroom), lighting becomes all the more important. By playing down one area and accentuating another, lighting can create a visual divider separating the business from its surroundings. In addition to presenting a more professional image, this makes it easier for you to tune out distractions when you're working.

The two basic kinds of lighting to choose from are incandescent lamps (bulbs) and fluorescent lamps (tubes). Each offers its own advantages, and the two types can be used separately or in combination.

Incandescent Lamps

Incandescent lamps are the most commonly used light source in homes. The lamp, or bulb, has the advantage of being small, with a beam of light that can easily light up a specific area. Particularly useful for illuminating desks and work tables, the incandescent light has a high degree of intensity. And, since its color is the standard by which other light sources are usually judged, people and merchandise generally look their most appealing under incandescent light. Special effects using colored bulbs are also possible. For instance, pink or yellow incandescent bulbs will make a room seem warmer and cozier. Blue and green bulbs have just the opposite effect, making it seem cooler and more spacious.

Fluorescent Lamps

Fluorescent lamps are especially good for lighting large areas. And, because they have a much longer life span, they are more economical than incandescent lamps. Whereas the typical incandescent bulb might last up to 4,000 hours, fluorescent tubes can be expected to last 18,000 hours or longer. To achieve the right lighting effect, though, proper selection of lamp colors is very important. The four most common colors of fluorescent lamps are:

Cool White. This produces the most light for your money. It makes rooms seem cooler and is especially good for displaying china, silverware, jewelry, and similar items. The lamp's one drawback, is that people and clothing do not look their best when illuminated by it.

Deluxe Cool White. Though 30 percent less efficient than cool white, this provides better color rendering of warm tones, thus making people look better. As a result, it's more suitable for general lighting needs.

Warm White. A predominantly yellow light, this produces a warm color that is closer to that of the incandescent lamp. In terms of cost and color quality, lighting experts often recommend it.

Deluxe Warm White. This light comes the closest to incandescent. It costs a little more than warm white, but if you want to make people and clothing look their best, it's the one to use.

WORKABLE FURNITURE

After you've organized the business in your mind and on paper comes the moment of truth—that time when you're ready to convert living space into working space and actually set up shop. Having tackled the challenges of maximizing space, increasing efficiency, and creating an image, all that's left is to find the furniture that works best for you.

The following types of furniture and accessories are all specially designed to maximize space. Ranging from the everyday to the exotic, each one is compact, versatile, and/ or portable.

- *Pull-out or tilt-out desk.* It folds into a bookshelf or wall unit when not in use.

- *Rolltop desk.* The rolltop keeps your work area covered when not in use.
- *Folding drafting table.* This can be stored flat until you need it.
- *Room divider–desk.* The desk is built into the room divider unit.
- *All-in-one work center.* Consisting of a desk, bulletin board, overhead storage area, and typing wing, this unit compresses everything into one small space.
- *Desk-top organizer.* This rests on top of your desk or hangs above it, providing additional storage space for supplies and papers.
- *Pool table-desk.* Probably the ultimate in home-based business furniture, this pool table has a sliding cover that enables it to be converted into a desk.
- *Lap board.* A portable desk that goes where you go, this takes up virtually no space whatsoever.
- *Folding chairs.* Available in wood or metal, these can be used at a desk or to provide additional seating when needed.
- *Portable filing cabinet on casters.* This can be pushed out of view when not in use.
- *Banker's-box spacesavers.* These are wall units with compartments for storing books, magazines, papers, files, catalogs, and forms.
- *Folding bookshelf on casters.* The bookshelf stacks against the wall or opens up into two or three separate units.
- *Pull-out sewing cabinet.* Sewing machine, work area, and storage space for patterns, fabrics, and accessories all fold into a wall cabinet.
- *Pull-out dining table.* This dining table pulls out to serve from two to eight people, but folds into a wall cabinet when not in use, thus creating more space for your business.
- *Bulletin board.* A business staple, this keeps messages and bits of paper from getting lost on your desk.
- *Pegboard with hooks.* This provides convenient storage for tools, scissors, thread, drafting materials, coffee cups, and more.

tools, scissors, thread, drafting materials, coffee cups, and more.
- *Ceiling hooks.* These can be used to display or store merchandise and supplies.

For information on buying computer equipment and software and on how your home-based business can benefit from the recent advances in office electronics, see Chapter 12.

Inexpensive Business Furnishings

If your goal is to furnish your business as inexpensively as possible, there are several ways to accomplish this without sacrificing style or efficiency. For starters, don't limit your shopping to furniture stores alone. Often you can find what you need for less money at hardware stores and shops specializing in building and artists' supplies. You should also investigate auctions, surplus outlets, and secondhand stores.

The government frequently sells used metal desks and filing cabinets for as little as $10 to $40 at public auctions. These can be easily restored and made to look less institutional by applying enamel paint to the metal surfaces. You might even build a desk or work table yourself by placing two filing cabinets parallel to each other and covering them with a large piece of Formica or wood that has been stained or painted. Industrial units made of bolted-together metal shelves and struts cost considerably less than wooden bookshelves and offer the advantage of being expandable. These shelves are perfect for displaying books or merchandise or for storing inventory. What's more, they can be painted to go with your color scheme. Cement blocks and boards can also be used to make inexpensive bookshelves. Or, you can build bookshelves using two ladders and boards. This is done by attaching the ladders to a wall at right angles, then suspending the boards between them, using the ladder rungs as supports.

TIPS ON FURNISHING
YOUR BUSINESS

1. Convert the hidden space in your home into working space.
2. Design the layout of your business so that those things you use most often are the closest to you.
3. Decide on the image you want to create before starting to furnish your business.
4. Use the Color Association Chart on page 61 to help determine which colors will work best for your type of business.
5. Make sure that the lighting is adequate and appropriate for your needs.
6. Save time and money by selecting furniture and equipment that can be easily maintained.
7. Look for furniture that is compact, portable, and capable of serving more than one function.
8. Don't make the mistake of overfurnishing your business space; more is not necessarily better.
9. Go to auctions and government sales to find bargains on furniture.
10. Pick up new ideas for furnishing your business and displaying merchandise by observing how other businesses do this.

6

Managing Your Time

As a home-based entrepreneur, one of the biggest challenges confronting you is learning how to make the best use of your time. No matter what talents or skills you possess, you cannot effectively utilize them unless you have the ability to manage your time. Thus, if your business is to achieve its potential, you will need to become adept at time management.

Benjamin Franklin's advice to a young tradesman, "Remember that time is money," has just as much relevance for business owners today as it did when he offered it in 1748. Time is one of the entrepreneur's most valuable resources. Moreover, time differs from other resources in that, once it's been spent, it can never be replaced. Unlike money or property, it can neither be borrowed nor bought; nor can it be stockpiled for use at a later date. But, by finding out where your time goes, identifying "time wasters," and setting priorities for what you want to accomplish in the time available, you *can* spend your time more profitably.

WHERE DOES THE TIME GO?

Before you can learn how to better manage your time, you must first ask yourself the all-important question, "Where does my time go?" Surprisingly enough, business owners who can easily account for the money they spend often find themselves at a loss when it comes to accounting for their expenditures of time. This is especially true of home-based entrepreneurs. Given the intermingling of work activities and personal activities that frequently occurs, home-based entrepreneurs are more likely to lose track of the time they spend on any one activity or project.

Keeping a Time Log

A useful technique for finding out where your time goes is to keep a daily record, or *time log*, detailing how you spend each waking hour in the day. By filling in a log similar to the one shown on page 69, you can easily determine the amount of time you spend on each activity. After several days of recording your activities in this way, you will have gathered a considerable amount of information about your current use of time. At this point, you should ask yourself these questions:

- What activities took up the greatest amount of my time?
- How important were those activities?
- Could I have eliminated any activities? If so, how?
- What things happened over which I had no control?
- Could I have handled those situations better?
- What were my biggest time wasters?
- What percentage of my time did I really spend productively?
- Did I accomplish the things I set out to do?
- How could I use my time more effectively?

As you may have discovered, time frequently does not go where it's supposed to go or where you think it has gone. Everyday interruptions (telephone calls, children's need for attention, deliveries), unforeseen occurrences (equipment breakdowns, uninvited guests), and emergencies (shipping delays, illness) have a way of eating into one's time. Another problem is simply the tendency of entrepreneurs (home-based and otherwise) to set unrealistic

DAILY TIME LOG   Date _____

How I Spent My Time

7:00 _____   3:00 _____

_____   _____

_____   _____

8:00 _____   4:00 _____

_____   _____

_____   _____

9:00 _____   5:00 _____

_____   _____

_____   _____

10:00 _____   6:00 _____

_____   _____

_____   _____

11:00 _____   7:00 _____

_____   _____

_____   _____

12:00 _____   8:00 _____

_____   _____

_____   _____

1:00 _____   9:00 _____

_____   _____

_____   _____

2:00 _____   10:00 _____

_____   _____

_____   _____

daily goals for themselves, fully expecting to accomplish two days' work in one day's time. This leads not only to workaholic behavior but to frustration as well. In this instance, instead of managing your time, your time is managing you.

The Maximum Time Available

Just how much time *is* available? Despite one's wishes to the contrary, the maximum amount of time available to anyone is 168 hours a week. This is a fact that even the best time-saving techniques and the most ingenious juggling of schedules cannot alter. Of that total, the number of hours you can actually use to run your business will depend on how much of your time is taken up by other activities. For instance, the hours in a typical week might be divided as shown on page 71.

In the event that you want to spend more than fifty-six hours each week on your business, then you will need to reduce the amount of time you spend on nonbusiness activities. Getting family members to share in the household duties or hiring outside help is one way to gain additional hours for your business. Spending less time on leisure activities is another. Or, if you can get by on less than eight hours of sleep a night, more hours can be freed this way. What might really be called for, though, is a change in your standards. This means accepting the fact that you can't always be the perfect housekeeper, gardener, gourmet cook, or anything else *and* be an entrepreneur. At times, given the demands of your business, you may have to put up with dust on the furniture, crabgrass in the yard, and takeout food on the table.

Of course you can spend less than fifty-six hours a week on your business, too. If you're working at an outside job, if you're busy meeting the needs of your family, or if you just want to spend more time on other activities, then the hours available for your business will be fewer. When the home-based business is a source of supplemental income, rather than the main source of income, owners are likely to spend only ten to twenty hours a week on the business.

```
 24  hours a day
× 7  days a week
168  hours a week

 56  hours spent sleeping
 14  hours spent eating
  7  hours spent on personal care
     (hygiene, exercise, grooming)
 14  hours spent on household activities
     (grocery shopping, cooking, cleaning, child
     care, home repairs, general maintenance,
     paying bills, etc.)
  7  hours spent on miscellaneous activities
     (meetings, doctors' appointments, shopping,
     etc.)
 14  hours spent on leisure activities
     (entertainment, recreation, socializing)
112  hours spent on nonbusiness activities
 56  hours available for your business. (If you have
     an outside job in addition to your home-based
     business, this time must be divided between
     both work activities.)
```

OVERCOMING TIME WASTERS

In going over your daily time log you will undoubtedly spot some time wasters—activities that took up your time but were ultimately unproductive. These include having your telephone call placed on hold, redoing a task that you did incorrectly the first time, engaging in a lengthy conversation with a neighbor, looking for a misplaced file. Depending on the nature of the time waster, it may be internally generated by you or externally generated by others or by events. An inadequate filing system that causes you to spend too much time looking for things is an internal time waster, since you can control it. However, waiting for your telephone call to be taken is an external time waster, because you have no control over it.

Internally generated time wasters are the easiest to eliminate because they are the result of your own actions. Once these actions are changed, the time waster disappears. Externally generated time wasters are more of a problem. Since these are beyond your control, you can't totally eliminate them and must sometimes simply accept them.

The first step toward eliminating or dealing with time wasters is to identify them. The chart on page 73 shows some of the most common ones. Having identified your time wasters, you can use these strategies to overcome them.

Strategies for Overcoming Time Wasters

1. *Organize your work environment.* Papers, files, supplies, and equipment should all be in their own special places and readily accessible when you need them. Instead of continually wasting time looking for misplaced messages and files, or walking extra steps to reach supplies and equipment, you must organize your work environment— now.

2. *Formulate objectives.* Formulating objectives for yourself and your business gives you something to shoot for, a direction to follow. Once your objectives are clear, procrastination and indecision should no longer be problems.

3. *Set priorities.* Instead of trying to do everything at once or spending too much time on unimportant activities, rank all your activities in order of their importance. Then focus first on those activities that have the highest priority. Low-priority items should be postponed until last, delegated to others when possible, or eliminated.

4. *Communicate clearly.* Just because something seems obvious to you doesn't mean it is obvious to others. Taking care to communicate clearly will save you time and money in the long run by reducing the number of time-wasting misunderstandings and mistakes that occur.

TIME WASTERS

Internal	External
Unorganized desk	Telephone interruptions
Inadequate filing system	Neighbors' visits
Inefficient work layout	Equipment breakdowns
Poor scheduling	Waiting for people
Procrastination	Lack of information
Lack of priorities	Needless meetings
Duplicated efforts	Excessive paperwork
Insufficient planning	Red tape
Failure to communicate	Incompetent people
Indecision	Misunderstandings
Spreading yourself too thin	Unclear policies and procedures
Inability to say no	
Unwillingness to delegate tasks	
Unclear objectives	

5. *Learn to say no.* The next time someone requests that you volunteer your services, stop and ask yourself a few questions: Is this something I really want to do? Would it be a good use of my time? Could someone else just as easily do it? This approach cuts back not only on time wasters but also on the stress caused by taking on too many responsibilities.

6. *Screen telephone calls.* If you are trying to meet a deadline or if you simply need some quiet time to yourself, use a telephone answering service or machine to screen your calls. You can quickly return those calls requiring your immediate attention and put off returning the less important calls until a more convenient time.

7. *Tell neighbors when you're working.* Politely but firmly explain to neighbors that your time for socializing is limited. Putting a Do Not Disturb sign on your door is one way to let others know that you are working. Some home-

based entrepreneurs even use flags or traffic signs (red means "No time to spare now"; green means "Come in and chat") to get the word out.

8. *Learn others' policies and procedures.* To ensure that your dealings with other businesspersons go as smoothly as possible, ask them to spell out their policies and procedures in advance. This will reduce misunderstandings and enable you to cut through red tape more quickly.

9. *Set time limits.* If clients keep you waiting or if you are spending too much time in meetings, let the people involved know that you must leave the meeting at a certain time. Using the excuse that you have another appointment should help to speed things along. Billing at an hourly rate is another possibility, giving clients the option of taking up less of your time or paying you for more of it.

10. *Keep equipment in good repair.* To avoid having equipment break down just at the moment you need it the most, establish a regular maintenance schedule for the equipment used in your business. As a further precaution, you should keep a list of numbers to call for emergency repairs or rental equipment.

SETTING PRIORITIES

In setting priorities for the things you wish to accomplish, it helps to use a *daily planner* similar to the one shown on page 75. Consisting of a "things to do" list, priority chart, and schedule, the daily planner enables you to rank your activities in order of importance and track the progress of each task through to completion. Activities that are not completed by the end of the day are carried over to the next day, the day after that, and so on until eventually they are either completed or eliminated.

The important thing to remember in organizing your time is that you should always give your attention to top-priority items first. Low-priority items can be tempting, especially when they are easier to do and take up less time, but it's a mistake to start with them. If you do, you may never finish the top- and high-priority tasks. So, instead

DAILY PLANNER

Date _____

Things to Do		Schedule
_____ _____		7:00
_____ _____		8:00
_____ _____		9:00
_____ _____		10:00
_____ _____		11:00
_____ _____		12:00
_____ _____		1:00

	Priorities	Comments/Status	
Top			2:00
			3:00
High			4:00
			5:00
			6:00
Med.			7:00
			8:00
Low			9:00
			10:00

of completing three low-priority items, you would do better to complete 20 percent of the work on one top-priority item.

Granted, setting priorities and sticking to them isn't easy. There will always be those days when everything cries out for your immediate attention and all of your projects should have been completed yesterday. But, as your time management skills improve, these days will become fewer and farther between.

SELF-MOTIVATION

The best time management system in the world will be of little use if you aren't motivated by the desire to succeed. To use your time well you have to *want* to accomplish something. During the start-up stage of your business, motivation isn't likely to be a problem. The challenge of getting the business established should be motivation enough to keep you going. But once the initial excitement begins to wear off, the need for self-motivation becomes more important.

Without someone—commonly known as "the boss"—to give you direction and reward your efforts, it's up to you to motivate yourself. This means coming up with new ways to generate energy and maintain the sense of satisfaction that you get from your business. Some of the techniques you can use to stay motivated include following your body clock, savoring your accomplishments, and setting new challenges for yourself.

Following Your Body Clock

A decline in motivation can sometimes be attributed to nothing more serious than trying to force your body to do something it doesn't want to do. Each person's body has its own natural timing mechanism that dictates when the body has the most energy, hence the tendencies of some people to be "day people" and others to be "night people." Since it's easier to change your schedule than your body clock, you should reserve your high-energy times for the high-priority items on your "things to do" list. This will enable you to accomplish more, which will in turn increase your motivation level.

Savoring Your Accomplishments

When you successfully complete an activity, meet a deadline, solve a problem, or make a sale, you should take time to savor your accomplishment. Instead of hurrying on to the next item on your list, you owe yourself a moment of self-congratulation. It doesn't have to be long—just time enough to say, "I did it." Instead of thinking of this as a waste of time or an indulgence, regard it as a basic need. Recognizing your own accomplishments and deriving satisfaction from them is one of the surest ways to stay motivated.

Setting New Challenges for Yourself

It's hard to stay motivated when you feel that the work you are doing is boring or unworthy of your talents. Fortunately, since you're the boss, you don't have to put up with this. To keep the excitement (and the profitability) in your business, set new challenges for yourself. Instead of getting stuck in an unbending daily routine, stop and ask yourself, "How can I do this better? Faster? More efficiently? What else can I do? What opportunities am I overlooking?" By rekindling your feelings of accomplishment, you will also rekindle your self-motivation.

BALANCING FAMILY AND BUSINESS NEEDS

At times, meeting the needs of your family and your business will probably seem like a juggling act. No matter how well thought out a home-based entrepreneur's schedule is, the unforeseen and urgent needs of family members (spouse, children, relatives) can easily throw it out of balance. This is true for all entrepreneurs, of course, but even more so for those who work at home.

There will also be occasions when your family resents your home-based business and its demands on your time. Before you established your enterprise, your family had exclusive rights to your time at home; now it must vie with the business for your attention. Under the circumstances, it's understandable that some family members may feel hurt or left out.

Despite these problems, it's still possible to have a successful home-based business, enjoy your work, and *not* alienate your family in the process. In addition to time management skills, you need an understanding of how family members feel about the business and the anxieties it might be causing them. You'll find it easier to balance the needs of your family and those of your business if you follow a few suggestions.

Make the business a joint decision. Rather than saying, "Here it is. This is my business. This is what I'm doing," discuss your idea for the business with family members. Let them know that their opinions and suggestions are important to you. You should also find out what misgivings, if any, they may have about the business. These can then be discussed and worked out in advance. In this way your family will be more likely to view your business as a welcome addition to your family life, rather than as an intrusion.

Get your family involved in the business. Your family won't seriously object to the demands that the business imposes on your time if it feels a part of what's happening. Whether or not you need help, or family members are willing to give it, you can still get them involved in your business by keeping them informed of your progress. New ideas, projects in the works, sales figures, and the goals you've set for the business should be shared with them. Remember, it will be easier for your family to care if you take the time to share.

Make it a learning experience. If you have children at home, try to make the business a learning experience for them. If they are old enough, and if they seem interested, your children may be able to help out in the business and learn at the same time. For the best results, (1) explain to your children that their work is important, (2) reward them for their time, and (3) make the business fun for them. Obviously, your goal is not to get free labor but to broaden your children's realm of experiences and let them feel a part of what you're doing.

Establish guidelines. To ensure that you will have sufficient time for your business and yet still be accessible to your family, establish guidelines for your working arrangement. For instance, set aside specific hours for business activities. At the same time, reserve specific hours to spend with your family. Explain that during business hours you should be interrupted only when absolutely necessary. Conversely, during family activities the business shouldn't be allowed to interrupt your time together.

Develop a support network. A support network consisting of baby-sitters, housekeepers, and the like can also help you to juggle your time. Help of this sort is especially important if you have small children whose needs for attention are pretty much constant.

Don't be too critical of yourself. Accept the fact that things will not always go as planned, and learn to live with that. Sometimes you won't get as much work done as you had hoped; other times you'll feel selfish for not devoting more time to your family. These are both to be expected and are part of the price you pay for the satisfaction of being an entrepreneur. In the final analysis, though, both your family and your business should profit from their exposure to each other.

TIME MANAGEMENT TIPS

1. Keep track of your time by using a daily time log.
2. Identify time wasters and develop strategies for overcoming them.
3. Set realistic daily goals for yourself.
4. Reserve your most productive times during the day for the high-priority items on your "things to do" list.

5. Take shortcuts whenever possible; for instance, a phone call is quicker than a letter.
6. Handle each piece of incoming mail one time only, making the decision as you read it to: Respond to it, file it, or throw it away.
7. Maintain your motivation and productivity levels by continually setting new challenges for yourself.
8. Fill out your daily planner the night before so that in the morning you can start right off with the first activity of the day.
9. Schedule "minibreaks" of ten to twenty minutes throughout the day to relax; then start your work again, refreshed.
10. Take a moment now and again to savor your accomplishments; you deserve it.

7

Promoting Your
Business

It isn't enough just to *be* in business. In order to succeed
in your home-based business you need to actively promote
it. A two-part process, this calls for you to identify potential
customers and develop an overall strategy for keeping
them informed about what your business has to offer..

FINDING YOUR CUSTOMERS

In the excitement of setting up your business, converting
living space into work space, and allocating your time, it's
easy to overlook one important factor—your customers.
All too often, new entrepreneurs wait until their businesses
are under way to sit down and determine exactly which
customers they hope to serve. At that point, it may be too
late. Having misjudged the marketplace, they find that
their businesses are already in trouble. So, to keep your
business from faltering before it has a chance to begin, it
is essential to identify your potential customers from the
start.

Here are some questions to ask yourself: Will your products or services be used primarily by adults or children?
Men or women? Married or single people? What income
level and age group will your customers come from? What

are their lifestyles? Are they politically conservative or liberal? Do they like to read? Jog? Cook? Travel?

The more you know about your customers, the better. This information will make it easier for you to reach them and fill their needs as well. This need for information also applies if you plan to sell to businesses rather than to individuals. In this instance, you'll want to learn as much as possible about what each business does, its individual requirements, budget limitations, and purchasing procedures.

To determine which people or businesses constitute your target market—the ones most likely to buy what you have to sell—you will have to do some marketing research. This means gathering customer information from some or all of the following sources:

• Personal observation
• The government
• Chambers of commerce
• Trade associations
• The media

Personal Observation

Keeping in mind the importance of looking before you leap, your marketing research should begin with your own personal observations of the field you are about to enter. For instance, suppose you were planning to design a line of greeting cards to be sold in gift and department stores. In this case, you would need to visit the stores themselves to see the types of people who shop there. Are they looking for humorous or serious cards? Cards for a special occasion or a general purpose? What styles and formats are the most popular? How much money are people willing to spend on a card? Which customers spend the most? In addition to answering these and other questions, your observations should also tell you how your product compares with those of competitors.

The Government

Government agencies at the federal, state, and local levels compile statistical data about consumer spending habits, sales trends, changes in the population, and so on. This information, which the government makes available to the public at little or no cost through reports and periodicals, can also help you to gauge the demand for your particular product. Those agencies offering the most useful information for identifying your target market include the Department of Commerce, the Small Business Administration, and the Economic Development Office. Most of the information you need should be in the reference section of your local library. You can also obtain it by writing to the specific agencies.

Chambers of Commerce

Your local chamber of commerce is another source of customer information that you should utilize. Established and operated by members of the business community, each chamber's goal is to promote and protect local business interests. As such, the chamber should be able to provide you with marketing research data pertaining to your particular business, along with help in formulating a workable promotional strategy.

Trade Associations

Trade associations, like chambers of commerce, can help you to get a better handle on your target market. Representing specific industries (arts and crafts, direct marketing, floristry, jewelry, real estate), trade associations provide industry members with a means of sharing ideas and information. Consumer profiles, forecasts of future demand levels and trends, and studies on the impact of proposed changes in government regulations are examples of the types of customer data available. To obtain information on trade associations or find out which ones represent your industry, write to the American Society of Association Executives, 1575 I Street, N.W., Washington, D.C. 20003.

The Media

The media (including newspapers, magazines, radio, and television) are vital channels of communication not only for promoting your business but also for obtaining information about your customers. Paying close attention to those articles and programs featuring or directed at your target market ("Women at Work," "Computer Update," "50 Dream Vacations," or whatever) should enable you to detect changes in the economy, customer needs, or current shopping patterns. What's more, following the advertisements is a good way to keep track of competitors' offerings and promotional strategies. Thus, one step in your marketing research should be to discover which media are most frequently used by your customers . . . and then tune in.

YOUR PROMOTIONAL STRATEGY

Once you have identified your potential customers you can begin to develop the promotional strategy for your business. In effect, this is a game plan for communicating with those individuals within your target market. Your goal is to get the word out about your products or services to as many potential customers as possible without exceeding your budget. This entails putting your resources of time and money to their most economical use. It also entails selecting those channels of communication (advertising and publicity) that are best suited for reaching your audience.

At the simplest, most direct level, your promotional strategy might consist of handing out business cards to people you meet and relying on the word-of-mouth comments of satisfied customers. In some instances—if you're in a very small town, for example, or if there is a great demand for what your business has to offer—this may be sufficient.

Normally, though, attracting customers to your doorstep will take more effort on your part. To meet the challenge you should be fully aware of the array of promotional tools at your disposal.

Advertising versus Publicity

The various tools you can elect to use in promoting your business come under one of two headings: advertising and publicity.

Advertising

Advertising involves the purchasing of time or space in the various communications media; it can be either institutional or product oriented. *Institutional advertising*, on the one hand, promotes your business in general, emphasizing its good name and any contributions it has made to the community. As a designer of greeting cards, for instance, you can use institutional advertising to emphasize your business philosophy: the desire to bring people together and help them say what they really want to say. *Product advertising*, on the other hand, promotes the specific products or services you sell, emphasizing the benefits associated with buying them from you. If you prefer to use product advertising, you can emphasize the greeting cards themselves and point out what makes them better than those produced by others.

Publicity

Publicity, though frequently confused with advertising, differs from it in these key areas: cost, control, and credibility. First of all, publicity—unlike advertising—is free. It doesn't entail the purchase of commercial air time or print space; rather, it involves getting information about your business or your products reported in the news media. Such coverage is provided free of charge when the information is thought to have news value or to be of interest to the public. However, just as there is no *cost* for the publicity you receive, neither do you have any *control* over its content. Unlike advertising, publicity can be favorable or unfavorable. A reporter is as likely to point out your business's problems as its accomplishments. If a news broadcast chooses to report on a lawsuit that's been brought against you instead of praising you for your volunteer service to the community, there's nothing you can do about it.

This lack of control is what gives publicity its greatest strength—*credibility*. The fact that it's the news media, rather than a sponsor, delivering your message makes it more believable than advertising.

Which is best, then—advertising or publicity? The answer is, both. In order for your promotional strategy to be really effective, it should use the tools from both categories. A promotional strategy that relies solely on advertising is missing out on the opportunity to get free media exposure for the business and thereby enhance its credibility. On the other hand, a strategy that relies on publicity alone to inform people about the business will lack continuity and control.

SELECTING ADVERTISING MEDIA

The advertising media generally favored by home-based businesspersons are the Yellow Pages of the telephone directory, direct mail, newspapers, magazines, flyers, and specialty advertising. Radio and television, though less popular because of the costs involved, are two other media alternatives.

Yellow Pages

Many owners of home-based businesses rely almost exclusively on the Yellow Pages section of the telephone book as a means of promoting their products or services. Adding to the appeal of Yellow Pages advertising is the growing number of specialty directories from which to choose— "The Neighborhood Directory," "Silver Pages," "Business to Business Directory," and so on.

The main advantage of Yellow Pages advertising is its ability to reach people in a specific geographic area (your neighborhood) at the time when they want to buy. Thus, the audience for your ad is presold. Having already decided what to buy, customers are just looking for the right place to buy it.

Given the presold nature of its audience, an ad in the Yellow Pages is essentially an attention-getting device. Your purpose is not only to provide information about what your business does but also to differentiate it from the competition. Here it's important to emphasize what sets you apart from the other businesses in your field— personalized service, unique products, next-day delivery, or whatever.

Depending on the size of your ad, Yellow Pages advertising can be an inexpensive way to promote your business on a year-round basis. However, this kind of advertising seems to work better for some businesses than for others. Those whose services are needed on short notice—such as florists, plumbers, and typists—tend to achieve the best results. Those who normally get their customers through referrals—accountants, marriage and family counselors, and free-lance editors, for example—usually do not fare as well. In any event, whether or not you decide to purchase an ad in the Yellow Pages, if you have a separate business phone in your home, you are still entitled to a one-line listing, free of charge.

Direct Mail

Direct mail, currently the third most popular choice with advertisers in general, is used by businesses large and small, home-based or otherwise. Consisting of letters, brochures, price lists, catalogs, coupons, and more, direct mail advertising is any material of a printed nature that is mailed directly to the intended customer. By way of advantages, it provides one of the best means of explaining and describing what your business sells. In addition to this, its flexibility enables you to send any message to anyone at any time. For instance, you can use direct mail to:

- Reach new customers
- Develop your image
- Inform customers of sales
- Introduce new products
- Announce price changes
- Solicit mail-order business
- Solicit phone-order business
- Maintain customer contact

Despite its obvious usefulness, though, direct mail has two drawbacks of which you should be aware. One, if you aren't careful, customers may regard your advertisement as junk mail and throw it away. Two, direct mail is one of the most costly forms of advertising per thousand persons reached, or CPM. In light of these drawbacks, your first concern in using direct mail should be to determine which potential customers are to receive your mailing. On this point marketing experts agree: More than any other factor—including the quality of the product, the words used to describe it, and the design value of the printed materials—the success of any direct mail campaign is largely attributable to its mailing list.

The Mailing List

How can you obtain the mailing list that's right for you? You can either build your own list or purchase one from someone else. In building your own list, you can rely on all or some of these sources: your present customers, your collection of business cards, telephone books, organization directories, newspaper announcements, and government records. To find those companies in the business of compiling and selling mailing lists, consult the *Standard Rate and Data Service*, a monthly publication available at many libraries. Regardless of your target market (women between the ages of eighteen and forty-five, skiers, recent graduates, personnel directors, purchasing agents), you will probably find an applicable list. The cost for this may be as low as $12 per thousand names or upwards of $300 per thousand.

Newspapers

Newspapers, traditionally the favorite advertising medium used by retailers, are another good means of promoting a home-based business. This is especially true when your target market is your own community. Since most papers are local, their readers are your potential customers. Along with this, newspaper costs can usually be tailored to meet even a very limited budget. Keeping your ad small or advertising in the classified section of the paper lowers the price. On the down side, however, it's important to remember that readers often overlook ads, skipping them entirely. And, since newspapers are rarely kept longer than a day or so, if your ad isn't read on the day it appears, it probably won't be read at all.

To heighten the effectiveness of newspaper advertising, many businesses specify that their ad appear in the section of the paper most likely to appeal to their customers (entertainment, business, sports, food, real estate). Thus, a caterer might place an ad in either the food or entertainment section. Although this *preferred positioning* costs more, it's certainly worth considering if it gets people to notice your ad. Offering a discount to those customers who mention seeing your ad in the paper or who redeem a coupon is another way to get more mileage out of newspaper advertising. It also tells you if your ad is working, since it allows you to measure readers' responses.

In debating whether or not newspaper advertising meets your needs, you should first contact the papers in your area. Ask them to send you a *rate card* and any *demographic information* describing their readers (by age, sex, marital status, income, occupation, and so on). This will tell you if ads in these papers will reach your potential customers at a price you can afford. It also will enable you to compare the costs per thousand persons (CPM) reached of the dif-

ferent papers. For example, if an ad in newspaper A costs
$600 and the same ad in newspaper B costs $650, it would
seem that the ad in newspaper A is the better buy. Yet,
when you take each paper's circulation into consideration,
you may find that the opposite is true.

$$\frac{\text{Cost of ad} \times 1,000}{\text{Total circulation}} = \text{CPM}$$

$$\text{Newspaper A} \; \frac{\$600.00 \times 1,000}{750,000} = 80\cent \text{ per } 1,000$$

$$\text{Newspaper B} \; \frac{\$650.00 \times 1,000}{850,000} = 76\cent \text{ per } 1,000$$

Magazines

Magazines, long used by major advertisers, are rapidly becoming an advertising staple among home-based business
owners as well. This is largely because of the continued
growth of special-interest magazines that focus on a single
topic (films, needlepoint, travel, skiing, gardening) and enable advertisers to reach a specific audience. Because these
magazines make it easier for you to pinpoint your target
market and because they normally charge less for ads than
do general-interest magazines, these publications are particularly valuable when your customers are spread out geo-
graphically.

Aside from putting you in touch with potential customers wherever they happen to be located, special-interest
magazines have other advantages. Like direct mail and
newspapers, they are well suited to conveying in-depth
information. And, taking those media one step better, since
people are inclined to read magazines in a leisurely manner
and save them afterward, magazine ads have a longer life
span.

Magazines have their disadvantages, too. One of these
is their *lead time*—the interval between the time your ad is
placed and the date it appears. Magazine ads usually must
be received two or three months prior to publication.

What's more, once your ad appears, there's no guarantee that readers will actually read it. Here, as with newspapers, positioning is important.

To find out which magazines cater to your potential customers and the advertising rates each one charges, consult a recent issue of *Standard Rate and Data Service* in your library. And, to get the best buy, don't forget to use the CPM formula to compare costs.

Flyers

A simple, inexpensive, and frequently effective tool for promoting your business is the flyer. Flyers can be printed in varying quantities and distributed to pedestrians, office workers, spectators at sports events, shoppers in supermarkets, attendees at trade shows, or other potential customers. This method of advertising not only enables you to reach your target market, but to do it on short notice as the need occurs. Since it isn't necessary to buy advertising space or obtain a mailing list, you can move quickly.

Before making your move, though, you should know the disadvantages of this advertising tool: Some people don't appreciate being given a flyer and won't hesitate to tell you so; others will throw your flyer away without looking at it; building supervisors and groundskeepers often discourage or even prohibit the handing out of flyers because of the litter they create. One way to get around these obstacles is to put together a professional-looking flyer with clean graphics and understandable copy. Another is to carefully select the people who are to receive it. For instance, participants in a 10-kilometer run should be likely prospects for a flyer advertising a physical fitness class . . . or chiropractor.

Specialty Advertising

Specialty advertising entails printing your business name, trademark, and/or a promotional message on any object given, free of charge, to potential customers. The object itself could be almost anything, as long as it's inexpensive and doesn't detract from your business's image. Calendars, pens or pencils, memo pads, bookmarks, magnets, luggage tags, caps, key chains, and T-shirts are just some of the objects used in specialty advertising.

This method of advertising could be particularly effective for you as a home-based businessperson, since it enables you to keep your name in front of your target market for an extended period of time. For instance, if you give out a calendar, your name might conceivably stay on a prospective customer's desk or wall for an entire year. With a T-shirt, not only does the recipient see your name for years to come, but so do others each time the shirt is worn.

The main difficulties in utilizing specialty advertising are in finding the right object to use (ideally it should relate to your products or services) and in distributing it to the right people. And, in the case of high-visibility objects like calendars and T-shirts, remember that looks count. A good design or catchy slogan is the key to future sales. Objects that are lacking in these areas just get thrown away.

Radio and Television

Because of their ability to reach large numbers of people, radio and television may also be of interest to you as a means of promoting your business. Be advised, however, that both media are complex forms of communication and that you will need a considerable degree of skill to use them properly. Knowing how to create an effective commercial and when and where to place it is an art in itself. Add to this the very high costs of radio and television advertising, and it becomes clear that you should study this area thoroughly before entering it. To find out more about radio and television advertising and whether or not it meets your needs and budget, consult the *Standard Rate and Data Service* in your library.

CAPITALIZING ON PUBLICITY

Although it's impossible to control the publicity you get, it *is* possible to influence it. The way to do this is by maintaining good press relations: providing timely and accurate information in the form of press releases; pointing out the angle that makes your story interesting or newsworthy; being available to answer questions; not making unreasonable demands. Once you've learned to work within the limitations of publicity, you'll be in a good position to take full advantage of it.

Creating a Press Release

Far from being anything mysterious, a press release is simply a fact sheet. Explaining who, what, where, when, and how, it states the details of the story you would like the press to tell. In so doing, it also tries to make the reporter's job easier by emphasizing *why* your story will be of interest to the public. Possible "whys" include: winning an award; giving a speech, presentation, or demonstration; having a unique product or service; staging a special event; helping a charitable organization. This story angle—or hook, as it's often called—is the most important information of all. Not only does this help to justify your story to the media, but it also tends to shape the kind of coverage you receive.

To give your press releases a professional look and increase their effectiveness, use the format shown on page 94.

BUSINESS CARDS AND STATIONERY

As a home-based businessperson, you should give special attention to your business cards and stationery. Along with selecting the design, color, and stock of paper that's best for each, you need to decide what information to put on them. Or, perhaps more important, you need to determine what information to omit. Here you should ask yourself, "How accessible do I want to be?" Being available is one thing; having customers ring your doorbell before breakfast, during dinner, or on your day off may be another. And what about strangers? Would you hand a stranger a piece of paper with your name, home address, and phone number on it? Definitely not, you say. Then stop and con-

---

PRESS RELEASE FORMAT

Contact: Your Name   Date

　　　　　Business Name

　　　　　Address

　　　　　Phone Number

Release Date (For Immediate Release; For Release
　after October 20, etc.):

Start copy here and begin with your angle: Why

Provide all necessary details: Who

　　　　　　　　　　　　　　　What

　　　　　　　　　　　　　　　Where

　　　　　　　　　　　　　　　When

　　　　　　　　　　　　　　　How

Write in short, clear sentences and paragraphs.
　Two pages should be the maximum length.

Double-space, using one-inch margins on all sides.

Put your name and phone number on each page.

Type "–30–" after the last line of copy to indicate
　the end.

–30–

---

sider whether or not you want your business cards im-
printed with this information.

　In addition to promoting your business, your cards and
stationery should also protect your privacy. Here are some
ways to accomplish this:

Business Cards. Use a post office box instead of your home address; indicate the city in which you reside, but exclude the street address; eliminate the address altogether and provide only a phone number; specify "By Appointment Only."

Stationery. Use a post office box instead of your home address; use your home address, but specify "By Appointment Only" on your letterhead.

Whatever methods you select, using your business cards and stationery to protect your privacy enables you to gain control over your time and to serve your customers in a more professional manner.

PROMOTION TIPS

1. Find out who your potential customers are; then learn as much about them as possible.
2. In determining which advertising media to use, select those that can most effectively reach your target market.
3. Maintain good press relations and put publicity to work for you.
4. Make it a point to join those organizations that can enhance your professional standing.
5. Keep your products or services in the public eye through guest speaking, demonstrations, and so on.
6. Create for your business a unique identity that sets it apart from competitors.
7. Get family members, friends, and colleagues to help spread the word about what your business has to offer.
8. Increase the visibility level of your business in the community by donating your time, products, or money to a local charity.
9. Ask your suppliers if they will help you pay for ads that feature their products (cooperative advertising).
10. Monitor your promotional efforts on an ongoing basis to keep track of what's working and what isn't.

8
Making the Sale

THE success of your home-based business rests largely on your ability to turn potential customers into satisfied customers. Even the best products and services aren't likely to sell themselves. First they need some assistance from you. Thus, having used your promotional strategy to get the word out about what your business has to offer, you must now use your selling skills to make the sale.

PREPARING TO SELL

Selling involves more than just giving a sales presentation and writing up an order (preferably a large one). To do it well takes preparation. Specifically, this entails locating new customers and tailoring your sales presentation to each individual's needs. These activities come under the heading of *prospecting* and *planning*.

Prospecting

"Prospecting" is the term salespeople use to describe the search for new customers. During this phase of the selling process your goal is to develop a list of potential customers, or "prospects," to whom you might sell your products or services. This encompasses such functions as:

- Identifying your prospects
- Contacting the prospects
- Collecting information about each prospect
- Maintaining prospect files
- Using current prospects to obtain leads to other prospects

The more good prospects you can develop the better. Whether you do all the selling for your home-based business or have employees or independent agents to help, your sales volume is dependent on prospecting.

Who Is a Good Prospect?

A prospect is any individual, group, or business that might be able to use what you have to sell. A *good* prospect, however, is something more than this. As shown in the chart on page 98 depicting your target market, a good prospect has three characteristics: (1) a need for your product, (2) the ability to afford it, and (3) the authorization to buy it. All three characteristics must be present. If any one of them is missing, your sale probably won't go through. Or if you make the sale, you may have difficulty in getting paid later.

You want to use your resources of time and money effectively. This means you shouldn't waste them trying to sell to bad prospects. Therefore, it's in your own best interest to obtain the answers to the following questions as quickly as possible.

Does the Prospect Need My Product? The most basic rule of selling is "Find a need and fill it." Taking this into consideration, your first priority should be to determine if a prospect has a need for your product or service. Will using it enable the prospect to save or make money? Increase efficiency? Look or feel better? Enjoy life more? Get respect from others? The greater the prospect's need for the purchase, the better your chances of making the sale. For instance, a health-conscious individual might have a need for nutritious foods, vitamins, exercise equipment, or membership in a health club, not to mention the proper

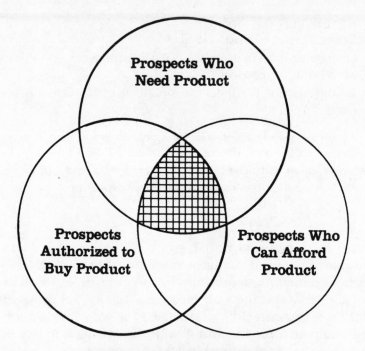

**YOUR TARGET MARKET
(GOOD PROSPECTS)**

clothing to show off his or her body. A business that wants to be more profitable might need anything from new equipment to a training program for its employees or an improved accounting system.

Can the Prospect Afford My Product? There's no point in trying to sell something to a prospect who is unable to pay for it. Much as the prospect might want or need what you have to offer, this alone isn't enough to justify your sales effort. Even if you succeed in making the sale, you could easily end up with nothing more than a bad debt to show for it.

The best way to protect yourself against losses from bad debts is to require that all purchases be made in cash or by cashier's check or money order. Accepting personal checks is riskier, but often an unavoidable part of doing business. You can reduce the risk by making sure that you get adequate identification from the prospect. As for extending credit to prospects, you would be well advised to have a credit reporting agency investigate the prospect's credit rating. To find the agencies in your area, look in the Yellow Pages section of the telephone directory under "Credit Reporting Agencies."

Is the Prospect Authorized to Buy My Product? In your eagerness to answer the first two questions, don't overlook this equally important one. Just because a prospect needs and can afford a product doesn't mean the prospect is authorized to buy it. For instance, a child may feel that he or she "needs" to see the horror movie playing at the local theater, and the child may even have the money to buy a ticket. But the actual authority to buy the ticket could very well rest with the child's parents, who have the final say on whether or not the movie is an appropriate one for the child to see. Married couples often share the authority to buy, especially when the purchase is a major one, such as a new home, new car, or new furniture. And, in selling to businesses, you'll find that the authority to buy can be spread out over different departments and levels of management. On important purchases it's not uncommon for as many as a dozen or more persons to be involved in the buying decision.

When more than one individual is involved in the buying decision it's usually better to have all parties present for your sales presentation. You should also try to determine which individual will make the final decision. This is the person to whom you want to direct the most attention during the sales presentation.

Maintaining Prospect Files

To keep track of your prospects you should have some kind of a filing system. This can be anything from separate sheets of paper held together in a binder to a computerized database. The system itself isn't what's important. Rather it's the customer information you've gathered and the ease with which you can gain access to it.

If your home-based business sells to other businesses,

the format for the entries in your prospect file might look something like the prospect file entry on page 101. In addition to the basic information (name, address, phone number, type of business), each prospect file entry should contain purchasing information and personal data. The purchasing information can be used to obtain reorders and to gain insight into the prospect's other purchasing needs. The personal data can be included in conversations with the prospect to establish a better working relationship.

Prospect files can be just as useful in selling to individuals as they are in selling to businesses. For instance, a travel agent can use prospect files to keep track of each customer's preferences regarding hotel accommodations, times of the year to travel, special interests, and budget requirements. A financial planner would want to maintain information on each prospect's savings, investments, and financial goals.

The time to start building your prospect files is when you begin to develop information about potential customers. At the outset, you might not have much more to go on than a prospect's name and an address or phone number. But as your relationship with each customer progresses, you'll be able to obtain additional information about the prospect's needs and buying habits. After each contact with the prospect (phone calls, letters, sales presentations), you should update your file entry to reflect any new information you have gathered.

Planning

The secret of a successful sales presentation itself is in the planning. Instead of "winging it" or relying on fast talking and fancy footwork to get through sales presentations, the best salespersons plan their presentations carefully. In so doing, you want to try to anticipate the prospect's needs, budget, and willingness to buy. Once you have a general idea of what products or services might appeal to the prospect, you can focus on preparing your presentation. Here you need to plan what to say and what visual aids or demonstration techniques to use.

PROSPECT FILE ENTRY	<u>Personal Data</u> Spouse's Name: _____ Children's Names: _____ Special Interests: _____ Activities: _____

Prospect Name: _____

Title: _____ Telephone: _____

Street Address: _____

City: _____ State: _____ Zip: _____

Type of Business: _____

Major Needs: _____

_____

_____

Competitors: _____

Credit Rating: _____

Product(s) Currently Used: _____

_____

Date of Last Visit: _____

Purchases Made: _____

_____

Terms: _____

Comments: _____

_____

_____

_____

Planning What to Say

In planning what to say in your sales presentation, your goal should be both to inform and to persuade. First, you want to provide the right amount and type of information so that the prospect knows what your home-based business has to offer. Second, you want to present this information as persuasively as possible so that the prospect will be inclined to buy your product or service. To achieve this end, it helps to do the following:

- Make a list of the major points you want to cover in the sales presentation.
- Determine the approximate length of time you will need to get your points across.
- Outline your presentation to see how everything fits together.
- Practice your presentation several times before actually trying it out on prospects. Recruit family members or friends to play the role of the prospect, and get their reactions.
- Don't try to memorize the presentation word for word. A memorized speech will have a stilted, unnatural sound and make it difficult for you to interact with prospects.
- In planning what to say, remember that it also pays to listen. This will enable you to create a more favorable impression and will help you determine the prospect's needs.

Using Visual Aids

Visual aids can make a sales presentation more interesting and help to hold the prospect's attention. Whether or not you decide to use them will depend on the nature of your product or service, the location where the presentation takes place, and your own preferences. The most obvious visual aid, of course, is the actual product that is for sale. Other visual aids include:

- Photographs
- Slides

- Filmstrips
- Blackboards
- Charts
- Maps
- Presentation folders
- Drawings
- Brochures
- Models
- Videotapes

In choosing visual aids, don't let yourself get carried away. If one visual aid is good, that doesn't necessarily mean that ten aids will be ten times as good. Too many visual aids can be both distracting and confusing. You're also better off keeping charts and graphs clean and simple, with a minimum of lettering or numbers on them. Otherwise they become difficult to read and end up hurting your sales presentation.

YOUR SALES PRESENTATION

When you've reached the point at which you're ready to face the prospect, you can strengthen your sales presentation by remembering to (1) communicate clearly, (2) appeal to the prospect's five senses, and (3) emphasize the benefits rather than the features of your product.

The Communication Process

The ability to communicate clearly is essential in giving a sales presentation. Before you can make the sale, you and the prospect must arrive at a meeting of the minds regarding what you are selling, its cost, the terms of the purchase, and so on. The only way for this meeting to take place is by communicating, or sharing ideas and information.

As shown in the diagram of the communication process on page 104, you must be able to get your sales points (messages) across to the prospect and properly interpret the prospect's reactions to them (feedback).

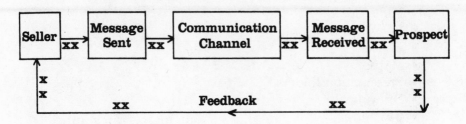

x = Noise

THE COMMUNICATION PROCESS

Sending the Message

In sending your messages, it's important to speak clearly and distinctly and to use words that the prospect is likely to understand. Try to avoid obscure words, jargon, and technical terms unless you are certain that the prospect is familiar with them. Don't overlook the nonverbal messages that you are sending, either. Otherwise, your body language (facial expressions, posture, gestures) could be telling the prospect something totally different from what you had planned. For example, slouching in your chair while telling a prospect about your attention to detail and insistence on quality will result in your sending two conflicting messages. Although your words are saying one thing, your body language is saying something else.

The Communication Channel

The communication channel itself is what brings you and the prospect together and enables you to send and receive messages to each other. This can be a face-to-face meeting between the two of you or a group meeting with several people in attendance. It can take place in a business setting, restaurant, home, or some other location. The communication channel can also be the telephone, a letter, or a fax. In the case of the telephone, though, since you and the prospect can't see each other, it's more difficult to send and receive messages. And with a letter or fax the communication process tends to be onesided. However, on the plus side, all of these communication channels are quick to use and don't involve any travel.

Interpreting Feedback

Once the prospect has received your message, it's up to you to interpret the feedback that is generated. Is the prospect's response to your message positive or negative? What questions are raised? What doubts or uncertainties exist? Is the prospect eager or reluctant to buy from you? Based on your interpretations of the feedback you receive, you can alter your sales presentation accordingly. The better you are at interpreting the prospect's messages, both verbal and nonverbal, the better you will be at making the sale.

Noise

The "noise" shown throughout the communication process refers to anything that interferes with the exchange of information between you and the prospect. This could be the sound of people talking, a ringing phone, or equipment being operated. It could also result from the way you send your messages (using a poor choice of words, speaking too softly, mumbling). Or it could stem from the way the prospect receives the messages (not hearing everything, daydreaming, misunderstanding what you said). Sometimes speaking louder or explaining a sales point in a different way can compensate for the noise. Other times you'll just have to do the best you can under the circumstances.

The Five Senses

One of the ways to increase the effectiveness of a sales presentation is to appeal to the prospect's five senses—the ability to hear, see, touch, smell, and taste. The more senses you can appeal to, the stronger your presentation will be. Instead of just talking to your prospects, you would do better to *show* them something. And if you can get a prospect to touch, smell, or taste your product, that's even better. Of course not every product or service can or should be made to appeal to all of the senses. You would hardly expect a prospect to taste the shoe polish you're selling or touch something unpleasant. But, by directing your sales presentation to those senses that your product does appeal to, you can improve your success rate in making the sale.

Food-related products and services are naturals for appealing to the five senses. A caterer shouldn't just describe the various dishes he or she prepares but should also show color photographs of them. Then, by giving the prospect a sample to taste, the caterer can allow the prospect to find out firsthand that the food tastes and smells as good as it looks. With some creativity, even seemingly difficult products and services can be made to appeal to the senses. Take insurance, for example. An agent can illustrate the need for insurance by showing prospects pictures of smiling policyholders whose home, car, life, or health insurance policies got them through misfortunes. A chauffeur, trying to sell prospects on the luxury of traveling in a limousine, might take them for a short ride. Professional speakers can offer prospects a chance to listen to audio cassettes of their talks . . . complete with applause.

Benefits versus Features

Emphasizing benefits rather than features is another way to strengthen your sales presentations. Whereas features describe a product or service, benefits are the advantages the prospect will derive from the purchase. The essential difference, as shown in the chart on page 107, is that benefits give the prospect a reason to buy.

Your role as the seller is to convert features into benefits. Instead of focusing on what a product or service is, you want to focus on what it can *do* for the prospect. Once you've done that, you'll find that there's less possibility of the prospect saying, "So what?" and a better chance that the response will be "That's great. I'll take it."

Features	Benefits
I provide a twenty-four-hour answering service.	You'll never miss any telephone calls again.
The exercise class consists of twelve lessons.	After twelve lessons you'll see a noticeable improvement in your muscle tone.
This is an original oil painting.	No one else will own a work of art like this.
I have the latest in word-processing equipment.	You'll get professional-looking typing at a reasonable price.
This ski parka is down-filled.	This parka will keep you warm on the ski slopes.
I use a carpet-cleaning machine that has deep foaming action.	Your carpets will look like new again.
As a press agent, I represent some of the biggest names in Hollywood.	I can get you on all of the television talk shows.
Our bed-and-breakfast inn is located near the ocean.	From your room you'll be able to see the ocean and hear the surf.
The stone in this ring is a genuine sapphire.	This sapphire ring brings out the blue in your eyes.
This house has a bedroom with an outdoor entrance.	This house has a bedroom that would make a perfect office for your home-based business.

Using the AIDA Formula

In giving sales presentations, many sellers find that it also helps to follow a formula—specifically the AIDA formula. Consisting of four steps, this sales formula is designed to get the prospect's attention and then move the prospect to take action (make the purchase). As you can see, the formula's name is derived from the first letter of each of the steps involved in using it:

A Attention: The seller strives to gain the prospect's *attention* and create an awareness of the products or services available.

I Interest: The seller stimulates the *interest* of the prospect by providing additional information.

D Desire: The seller arouses the prospect's *desire* to purchase the product or service by emphasizing its benefits.

A Action: The seller encourages the prospect to take *action* and buy.

Like shifting from one gear to another when driving a car, the transitions between steps in the AIDA formula should be smooth and natural. Once you've succeeded in getting the prospect's attention, you can begin to explain exactly what your home-based business has to offer. Having made this clear, your next step is to show how your products or services can fill the prospect's needs. And last of all, when everything's been said and done, you should help the prospect make the final buying decision.

HANDLING OBJECTIONS

Many sales experts insist that "the selling doesn't really begin until the customer says no." Instead of letting objections upset you or taking them personally, you should try to maintain a positive attitude. Accept the fact that your prospects' objections come with the territory. All sellers encounter them at one time or another. What separates the successful sellers from the rest is how they handle these objections.

Some of the most common objections prospects raise during sales presentations include:

1. I don't really need it right now.
2. I can't afford it.
3. Your price is too high.
4. I need more time to think about it.
5. This isn't what I had in mind.
6. I always buy these from another company.

Any one of these objections can effectively put an end to your sales presentation—if you let it. But by responding to the objection in a positive way and demonstrating that the benefits of the purchase outweigh the disadvantages, you still may be able to make the sale.

The following examples show how you can turn objections into orders:

1. *I don't really need it right now.* If the prospect doesn't need what you are selling, there's nothing more to talk about, right? Not necessarily. Instead of accepting this objection at face value, try to determine whether or not a need really does exist. If, in your opinion, the prospect *does* need what you have to offer, then point this out:

"I understand that you already have insurance coverage. But your current policy doesn't provide any protection against damage from floods or rock slides, which occur often in this part of the country. For the same price, this policy provides you with full coverage against such possibilities."

2. *I can't afford it.* Ordinarily there is no point in continuing your sales presentation if the prospect really can't afford your products or services. However, if you're confident that the prospect *can* afford to buy, then you should explain how:

"Your reluctance to use a bridal consultant isn't surprising. After all, weddings these days are expensive. But can you really afford to leave anything to chance on this once-in-a-lifetime occasion?"

3. *Your price is too high.* This is a common objection voiced by prospects. But if you know for a fact that your price is in line with those of your competitors, draw this to the

prospect's attention. On the other hand, if your price *is* higher, then discuss the reasons for this:

"Yes, it's true that my prices are higher. That's because I use only the finest ingredients, and there are no preservatives in any of my cookies or cakes."

4. *I need more time to think about it.* When a prospect raises this objection, your job is to find out *why* the prospect needs more time to make a decision. If the delay seems justified, you should go along with it and set up a specific date to get the prospect's answer. But if you think the prospect is really saying no, then emphasize the benefits again:

"I realize it isn't every day that you decide to reupholster your furniture. Fortunately, this fabric you like is on sale, so that will save you money. What's more, if we go ahead and write up the order now, you can have the sofa and chair back in time for the holidays."

5. *This isn't what I had in mind.* Overcoming this objection can be a definite challenge, especially if you don't have anything else to offer the prospect. Don't give up, though. Find out what the prospect doesn't like about the product or service you are selling; then try to turn these disadvantages into benefits:

"The house *is* small, but that's what makes it so perfect for an active couple like you. It's virtually maintenance-free. So you won't have to spend your weekends cleaning or doing yard work."

6. *I always buy these from another company.* Even the most loyal customer can usually be swayed by a better offer. The best way to counter this objection is to prove that it will be more profitable for the prospect to buy from you:

"Your loyalty is commendable. However, let's take a look at what your profit margin will be if you order your T-shirts from me. Don't you owe it to yourself at least to try them in your store?"

CLOSING THE SALE

If the prospect is responding favorably to your presentation and appears ready to make a decision, just one thing remains—closing the sale. This is the moment when you actually ask the prospect to buy.

There are several ways to close a sale. The most frequently used methods include (1) asking for the order; (2) assuming the prospect will place the order; (3) giving the prospect a choice; (4) providing an added inducement to buy; and (5) warning the prospect to buy before it's too late.

Asking for the Order

The simplest, most direct way to close a sale is to ask the prospect to place an order. Rather than beating around the bush or backing into the close, this approach meets it head on:

- "Would you like me to go ahead and write up your order now?"
- "Now that you know what my service is all about, shall we go ahead and schedule an appointment?"

The best time to use this closing technique is when the prospect already seems sold on making the purchase. The main drawback of this method is that, if the prospect says no, there's very little you can do to turn the situation around.

Assuming the Prospect Will Place the Order

Instead of asking if the prospect is interested in buying, this approach *assumes* that the sale already has been made:

- "If you'll just fill in this information, I'll finish writing up your order."
- "I agree with you that these are beautiful. They'll look perfect in your living room."

This closing technique is particularly successful when the prospect wants to buy but is reluctant to make the decision to go ahead. Since you have, in effect, made the decision for the prospect, there's no further obstacle. Beware, though, in using this technique. You don't want to put too much pressure on the prospect. If you do that, you can cause the sale to fall through.

Giving the Prospect a Choice

In this method of closing, the seller asks the prospect to choose which of two or more alternatives is preferable:

- "Do you prefer the blue or the green?"
- "Would you rather have it delivered on Monday or Tuesday?"

The advantage of closing with a choice is that this makes it much easier for you to avoid a no answer. And by choosing one alternative over another, the prospect is essentially closing the sale for you.

Providing an Added Inducement to Buy

This closing technique sweetens the pot by offering the prospect an added inducement (price discount, early delivery, extra service, and so on) to buy your product or service:

- "If you agree to place your order today, I'll pay for the shipping charges."
- "Normally my fee would be two-hundred and fifty dollars for a project this size. But if we can work out the details today, I'll only charge you two hundred."

The added-inducement close may indeed result in a sale, but it lowers your profit, so you should use it sparingly.

Warning the Prospect to Buy

This approach to closing can best be described as the don't-miss-the-boat strategy. By warning the prospect to buy before it is too late, the seller adds a sense of urgency to the purchase:

- "These are the last ones I have in stock. To guarantee delivery I need to receive your order today."
- "Houses in this area rarely stay on the market for long.

I recommend that you put in an offer on this one before someone else does."

Although this technique is quite often successful, you should limit its use to those times when the product or service you are selling is in short supply. Otherwise you run the risk of developing a reputation for using high-pressure tactics.

SALES TIPS

1. Make a point of prospecting for new customers on an ongoing basis; the more good prospects you can develop the better.
2. Don't waste your time trying to sell to unlikely prospects; focus on the ones in your target market.
3. Set up a prospect filing system to keep track of potential customers.
4. Remember that the secret of a successful sales presentation is careful planning.
5. In giving your sales presentation, communicate clearly, appeal to the five senses, and emphasize the benefits of your product or service.
6. Don't get so caught up in the presentation that you forget to interpret the prospect's feedback.
7. Use the AIDA formula to gain the prospect's attention and move the prospect to buy.
8. Be prepared for the prospect's objections; proper handling can turn these into sales orders.
9. Don't let the prospect put you on the defensive; it's easier to deal with objections when you maintain a positive attitude.
10. Remember to ask for the order; to make the sale, you have to close.

9

Pleasing Your Customers

THE selling process doesn't stop when the sale is made. In many ways this is just the beginning. Once you've made the sale, your real challenge is to keep the customer. If you want to encourage repeat sales, you must realize that the number one priority of your home-based business should be pleasing your customers.

Considering the time and money that go into developing prospects and convincing them to buy, it makes sense to maintain good customer relations. After all, it's easier to sell to a customer who's already sold on your business than it is to sell to someone who doesn't know anything about you. This explains many businesspeople's claims that "After the sale we don't forget the service."

Pleasing the customer takes on even greater importance to you as a home-based business owner than it might to someone else, because customers tend to expect more personal service from home-based businesses. Furthermore, home-based businesses often rely heavily on the word-of-mouth comments of satisfied customers, so this is another reason to please your clients.

YOUR ROLE AS MATCHMAKER

To achieve your goal of pleasing the customer, it helps to think of yourself as a matchmaker, matching your products and services with the needs of the customer. The more skillfully you are able to make the match, the more profitable your business will be on both a short-term and a long-term basis. The results of good matching are (1) satisfied customers, (2) continued patronage, and (3) customer referrals.

Satisfied Customers

You should make a distinction between satisfying your customers and selling to them. Since you get paid in both instances, the difference might not seem important. But it is. Many businesses start out strong, rapidly showing a profit and steadily increasing their sales volume. Then, seemingly without warning, things start to go wrong. Sales drop and soon the businesses are fighting for their own survival. Why? What causes this to happen? It happens because the businesses were not really trying to meet the needs of their customers. They were more interested in "moving the goods" or "pushing services" . . . whether or not customers really needed them.

On a short-term basis a strategy that emphasizes selling over satisfying might seem like the way to go. It's quicker and easier, and the results can be readily seen on an income statement—for a while. On a long-term basis, though, satisfying your customers is what counts the most. Building a reputation for quality and service is what ultimately will enable you to *stay* in business.

Continued Patronage

The lifeblood of any business is the continued patronage of its customers. In addition to making the sale, you want to keep the customer coming back for more. When this happens and you develop a loyal following of customers who regularly patronize your home-based business, you have what is known as a *customer franchise*. This can be one of your most valuable business assets since it represents virtually a presold market for your products and services. Proof of the value of a customer franchise is the fact that when a business is sold its purchase price is usually determined by the number of customers who regularly patronize it. The more active customer accounts the business has, the higher the purchase price.

Customer Referrals

Building a loyal following of customers for your home-based business means not only increased sales but increased customer referrals as well. When customers are pleased with the products or services they receive, it's only natural that they want to recommend them to others. This positive word-of-mouth publicity can cause your customer accounts to expand at an accelerated rate. For example, take a look at what happens when each of ten satisfied customers recommends your service to two other people who, in turn, tell two others, who tell two more . . .

$$
\begin{array}{rl}
10 & \text{Satisfied customers} \\
\times\ 2 & \text{Others (friends, relatives, colleagues)} \\
\hline
20 & \text{New prospects} \\
\times\ 2 & \text{Others} \\
\hline
40 & \text{New prospects} \\
\times\ 2 & \text{Others} \\
\hline
80 & \text{New prospects}
\end{array}
$$

$$10 + 20 + 40 + 80 = 150 \text{ Total prospects}$$

What started out as ten satisfied customers has mushroomed into a group of potential customers fifteen times that size . . . and still growing. The reason for this growth is that, rather than merely doubling the number of prospects for your products and services, word-of-mouth publicity multiplies it, creating a pyramid effect.

In addition to illustrating the importance of positive word-of-mouth publicity, this should also serve as a warning not to alienate your customers. Negative word-of-mouth publicity travels just as far and can have devastating consequences for a business. The best way to guard against it is to maintain good customer relations.

MAINTAINING GOOD CUSTOMER RELATIONS

Maintaining good customer relations consists of helping customers to get the full benefits from their purchases. Beyond delivering what the customer paid for, it involves providing that "something extra" that's often necessary to ensure that the customer's needs are fully satisfied. Although each business is different, the most common methods for maintaining good customer relations include:

- Expediting the purchase
- Providing personal service
- Answering questions
- Handling complaints
- Solving problems
- Staying in touch with customers

Expediting the Purchase

Once the customer has agreed to buy your product or service, the focus of your energy should shift from making the sale to completing the transaction. This means doing everything possible to expedite the purchase by (1) reassuring the customer that the purchase is the right one, (2) speeding delivery of the goods, and (3) overseeing any installation or implementation that may be required. Something as simple as telling the customer, "You'll get a lot of use out of that" or "You made a wise decision" can go a long way toward relieving any anxiety associated with the purchase. So can making sure that there are no delays in getting your product into the customer's hands or in performing the service that the customer expects. Nothing is more frustrating for a customer than deciding to buy something and then having to wait longer than necessary for the seller to deliver it. In conjunction with this, if your business is supposed to install or implement the product (computer equipment, home remodeling, landscaping), it's your responsibility to see that the job is done correctly.

Providing Personal Service

Personal service may, in fact, be the best customer-relations tool of all. With the growth of huge conglomerates, chains, and self-service outlets, personal service has become an endangered species. Customers who want to be treated as individuals are more likely to receive "cookie cutter" service that treats all customers the same. In light of this situation, if your home-based business provides the kind of personal service that is lacking elsewhere, this gives you the edge. The increasing number of bed-and-breakfast inns located throughout the United States provide a prime example of this. Rather than patronizing a hotel or motel, many travelers are choosing to stay at small B-and-B's. Here, in place of color television sets, they are finding uniquely furnished rooms, home-cooked meals, and attentive innkeepers eager to make their stay memorable.

Regardless of what type of business yours is, you can make it better by providing customers with personal service. You can accomplish this by addressing each customer by name, taking individual preferences into consideration, providing choices whenever possible, and doing more than is expected. Since these "little things" often mean a lot to customers, paying attention to them puts your business at a distinct advantage over those businesses that ignore them.

Answering Questions

Being available to answer questions after the purchase has been made is essential for good customer relations. It gives customers a sense of security to know that if they need additional information or instructions they can always call you. This adds to the customer's satisfaction and helps keep minor problems or misunderstandings from becoming big ones. And by keeping the lines of communication open, you stand a better chance of making more sales in the future. Thus, instead of avoiding customers' questions or viewing them as time wasters, think of them as new opportunities to sell customers on your business and what it has to offer.

Handling Complaints

Part of your customer-relations effort, by necessity, must be directed at handling complaints. Just as customers can be expected to voice objections during sales presentations, they can also be expected to voice complaints after the sale is completed. Complaints are a fact of business life. The issue isn't really who's right or who's wrong, but what needs to be done to satisfy the customer. Whenever a customer raises a complaint, your first concern should be to get to the heart of the problem as quickly as possible. If there is something wrong with your products or services, you want to determine what you can do to improve them. If a customer is unhappy with a purchase, you must decide how you can remedy the situation. Whatever the reason for a complaint, your sincere effort to resolve it will enhance the reputation of your business and lead to positive word-of-mouth publicity.

Solving Problems

The most successful sellers are problem-solvers. After they make a sale, they go out of their way to help their customers put the products or services to the best use. If a problem comes up, instead of saying, "That's not my job," successful salespeople are willing to work with their customers to find a solution. When you do these things, you let customers know that you're on their side and are ready to use your expertise to help solve any problems they are experiencing. For instance, an acting instructor might advise students where to get professional-quality, eight-by-ten-inch glossy photographs taken or how to find a talent agent. A bait seller could help customers by telling them where the best fishing spots are located.

CUSTOMER RELATIONS EVALUATION FORM

	Answer yes or no
1. My selling strategy is oriented toward satisfying each customer.	_____
2. I work hard to encourage the continued patronage of customers rather than just to get the sale.	_____
3. I try to generate positive word-of-mouth publicity.	_____
4. My goal is to establish long-term customer relationships.	_____
5. I try to get to know each customer as an individual.	_____
6. I always provide personal service.	_____
7. I address each customer by name.	_____
8. I make a point of staying in touch with customers.	_____
9. When a customer has a question, I try to answer it as quickly as possible.	_____
10. I handle complaints courteously and efficiently.	_____
11. I am willing to work with the customer to solve any problems that come up.	_____
12. Once I have made the sale I try to expedite the delivery.	_____
13. I spend part of my time reassuring my customers.	_____
14. I like to give each customer something extra rather than just the bare minimum.	_____

Staying in Touch with Customers

Business owners can also bolster their customer relations by staying in touch with customers on a regular basis. Instead of waiting for customers to contact you, take the initiative yourself. Telephoning from time to time to see how customers are doing is one way to accomplish this. Sending a card or a small gift to each customer at Christmas is another. Or you might send out a mailing to provide customers with up-to-date information about your products or services. And, of course, when you make a new sale it never hurts to send the customer a thank you note.

RATING YOUR CUSTOMER RELATIONS

To make sure that you are doing everything possible to please your customers, use the Customer Relations Evaluation Form on page 120 to rate yourself.

CUSTOMER RELATIONS TIPS

1. Remember that it's easier to sell to your current customers than to people who don't know anything about you.
2. Think of yourself as a matchmaker, matching your products and services with the needs of the customer.
3. Don't forget that the most valuable asset of your business is its customers; the customer always comes first.
4. Good customer relations are built on providing quality and service to the customer.
5. Don't overlook the power of word-of-mouth publicity; this can make or break a business.
6. Let customers know that you appreciate their patronage; take the time to say thank you.
7. After you have made the sale, be sure the customer receives your product or service as soon as possible.
8. Don't take the money and run; being available to answer questions or handle complaints is essential for good customer relations.

9. Treat each customer as an individual; providing personal service will help your business grow.
10. Make it a point to stay in touch with customers; frequent follow-up calls or letters will enable you to meet each customer's current and future needs.

10

Getting Ready for April Fifteenth

THE easiest way to get ready for April fifteenth is by keeping good records throughout the year. The more accurate and up to date your financial records are, the simpler it will be to prepare your tax returns. Good records enable you to substitute facts for guesswork, continuity for confusion. And in addition to depicting the financial history of your home-based business, they provide a scorecard you can use to rate its performance.

WHY RECORDKEEPING IS SO IMPORTANT

It is important to keep good records to satisfy the government, but you also need them for your own benefit. By taking the time to set up and maintain a recordkeeping system for your business, you will ensure that you receive all of the business-related tax deductions you have coming to you. Furthermore, your records can be a valuable tool in making business decisions and in helping you to identify problems quickly and take corrective action. Instead of having to hunt for financial information or develop it on the spot, you already have it in hand waiting to be used.

For example, an efficient recordkeeping system should give you this information:

- Monthly sales totals
- Taxable income for the year
- Amount of money invested in inventory
- Business operating expenses
- Products or services most in demand
- Sales made on credit
- Customers behind on their bills
- Financial obligations coming due

These facts, which are necessary for tax reporting and management purposes, also may be required by any suppliers or lending institutions with whom you do business.

CHOOSING THE BEST SYSTEM

The Internal Revenue Service does not stipulate what kind of records a business owner must keep, only that the records properly identify the business's income, expenses, and deductions. Thus, as a home-based businessperson, you may use any recordkeeping system that meets this criterion and is suited to your business. For best results, the recordkeeping system you choose should be 1) simple to use, 2) easy to understand, 3) accurate, 4) consistent, and 5) capable of providing timely information.

You can choose from among a number of business recordkeeping systems, ranging from simple to complex. The simplest of these are the single-entry and pegboard systems; the most complex is the double-entry system.

Single-Entry Recordkeeping System

The single-entry recordkeeping system is based on your income statement rather than your balance sheet. Thus, unlike the double-entry accounting system, it does not require you to "balance the books" or record more than one entry for each transaction. The simplicity of the system is its best feature and the one that makes it so appealing to the owners of new or small businesses. For tax purposes, the system enables you quickly and easily to record the flow of income and expenses generated by your business. In addition to this, a good single-entry recordkeeping system provides a means of keeping track of your accounts receivable, accounts payable, depreciable assets, and inventory.

For help in setting up a single-entry recordkeeping system specifically tailored to the needs of your home-based business, consult an accountant or bookkeeper. Or you may find that one of the commercially available ready-made systems is sufficient for your needs. Generally consisting of worksheets bound together in a spiral notebook, these systems can be purchased for less than $15 at office-supply and stationery stores. The most popular single-entry system is the one put out by Dome Publishing Company.

Pegboard Recordkeeping System

The pegboard recordkeeping system is actually a single-entry system since it requires only one entry per business transaction. But its design and the way you use it put it in a category by itself. For one thing, it is an all-in-one system that not only keeps track of your records but also provides the materials for writing checks and issuing receipts. The system derives its name from the fact that the checks and receipts it uses are overlaid, one after another, on top of your permanent record sheets and held in place by pegs. Whenever you write a check or receipt, the information is automatically transferred, via carbon paper, to the record sheet below. This is the system's most distinguishing feature because it eliminates the cause of the majority of recordkeeping errors—forgetting to enter a transaction in the books.

The price of a pegboard system can range from $75 to $200, depending on the system's size and complexity. This includes the printing costs for personal checks and receipts. Consult the Yellow Pages under "Business Forms and Systems" for the pegboard system specialists near you.

Double-Entry Recordkeeping System

The double-entry recordkeeping system is more involved than the single-entry and pegboard systems. But, because of its built-in checks and balances, it provides greater accuracy and may be better suited to your business. Based on the balance sheet rather than the income statement, it requires that two entries be made for every transaction that is recorded. This is based on the fact that all business transactions involve an exchange of one thing for another. For instance, if a customer buys merchandise from you and pays cash for it, the amount of money in your business increases while at the same time the inventory level decreases. Under the double-entry system, you must record both changes in your books—one as a debit entry and the other as a credit entry. This is where the checks and balances come in: For each transaction, the total debit amount must always equal the total credit amount. If the amounts are out of balance, the transaction has been improperly recorded.

Unless you have had some bookkeeping or accounting experience, you will probably need help to set up and maintain a double-entry system. Many home-based entrepreneurs have a bookkeeper come in once a week or once a month, as needed, to do their books. One way to find a part-time bookkeeper is to call the colleges in your area and ask if any students majoring in accounting are seeking work experience. Or perhaps there is a home-based bookkeeping service nearby that can meet your needs.

RECORDING YOUR INCOME

One of the most important functions of your recordkeeping system is to provide an accurate record of the sources and amounts of income generated by your business. This is essential not only for tax-reporting purposes but for decision-making purposes as well. At the bare minimum, the income records for your home-based business must include a cash receipts journal. If you extend credit to your customers, you will also need an accounts receivable journal.

Cash Receipts Journal

The cash receipts journal below illustrates how a business (in this case a word processing service) can simply and easily keep track of its income flow. Recording the date, source, and amount of income earned, the cash receipts journal also indicates which services are most in demand. Thus, in addition to providing you with the income figures required by the Internal Revenue Service, it provides valuable information about your target market. After a few months of recording your cash receipts in this way, you should know who your best customers are and which products or services are your best sellers.

The owner of the word processing service specializes in four different kinds of typing: legal briefs, manuscripts, student theses, and medical transcriptions. Yet, the cash receipts journal shows that the income from legal briefs far exceeds the income from any one of the other services.

ABC ENTERPRISES
APRIL 19XX
CASH RECEIPTS JOURNAL

DATE	DESCRIPTION/NAME	LEGAL BRIEFS	MANUSCRIPTS	THESES	TRAN-SCRIPTIONS
4/3	DR. JOHN LEWIS				300 00
4/6	ATTY. EILEEN FERRIS	275 00			
4/8	WILLIAM SMITH		350 00		
4/12	ATTY. NANCY MILLER	300 00			
4/16	ATTY. JOSEPH BROWN	150 00			

This is a good example of what marketing experts call the 80/20 Rule. According to the rule, 80 percent of a business's sales are likely to come from 20 percent of its customers (attorneys in this instance). These are your best prospects, the ones who can most benefit from your products or services. As such, once you've identified them, you should direct your advertising, selling, and customer relations efforts toward filling their needs.

Accounts Receivable Journal

Whenever possible, customers should be required to pay for their purchases at the time the sale is made. This gives you the immediate use of the funds and eliminates the need to collect them later. However, if it's necessary to allow your customers to buy on credit, then it's vital that you maintain an accounts receivable journal similar to the one shown below. This will provide a record of each sale and enable you to keep track of the money that is owed you. Then, when you receive payment, you can enter the income in your cash receipts journal.

ABC ENTERPRISES
ACCOUNTS RECEIVABLE JOURNAL

DATE DUE	DESCRIPTION/NAME	DATE REC'D	AMOUNT DUE	30 DAYS PAST DUE	60 DAYS PAST DUE	90 DAYS PAST DUE
3/15	GREG ADAMS		300 00	✔	✔	
4/21	HARRY DAVIS	4/20	400 00	⊢	⊢	⊢
4/30	JEAN BROWNING	4/30	250 00	⊢	⊢	⊢
5/17	MARY DECKER		325 00			

BUSINESS EXPENSES

The recordkeeping system for your home-based business must provide you with a record of tax-deductible business expenses. For it to do this, you will have to determine precisely what expenses legitimately can be termed "business expenses." As explained in Chapter 1, the Internal Revenue Service regards as deductible only those expenses that are "ordinary in your business and necessary for its operation." Here are just a few of the expenses that meet these criteria:

- Accounting services
- Advertising
- Attorney's fees
- Automobile
- Business publications
- Charitable contributions
- Club dues
- Consultants' fees
- Credit reports
- Depreciation
- Entertainment
- Freight charges
- Insurance
- Interest
- Licenses
- Maintenance
- Materials
- Messenger service
- Newsletters
- Postage
- Publicity
- Rent
- Safe deposit box
- Salaries
- Sales commissions
- Stationery
- Supplies
- Taxes
- Travel
- Utilities

In calculating your business expenses it's important to separate them from your personal expenses. For instance, travel expenses on a business trip are deductible, but the same expenses on a vacation are not. Taking a client to lunch is deductible; going to lunch with a friend purely for social reasons is not. Postage on Christmas cards sent to customers is deductible; postage on the cards sent to friends and relatives is not. In the event that an expense is partly for business and partly personal, only the business part is deductible. For example, if you go on a trip for both business and pleasure, you can deduct only the business portion of the trip.

Cash Disbursements Journal

The best way to keep track of your expenses is to enter them in a cash disbursements journal like the one shown below. In so doing, make sure to record the following information:

- Date the expense was paid
- Name of person or business receiving payment
- Check number
- Amount of check
- Category of business expense

When you set up your expense categories, arrange them in either alphabetical order or the order in which they will appear on your tax forms. This will make it easier for you to locate the information later and transfer it to your tax forms when preparing your income tax return. At the end of each month it's also a good idea to add up the expenses in each category to determine exactly where your money is going. This should help you to stay within your budget and keep unnecessary expenses to a minimum.

ABC ENTERPRISES
APRIL 19XX
CASH DISBURSEMENTS JOURNAL

			1	2	3	4
DATE	DESCRIPTION/NAME	CK #	ACCOUNTING	ADVERTISING	AUTOMOBILE	UTILITIES
4/3	JOE LOUIS, C.P.A.	645	650 00			
4/7	DAILY TIMES	646		400 00		
4/9	AUTO DEALER	647			75 00	
4/13	ELECTRIC COMPANY	648				45 00

Home Business Expenses

Because you do business at home you may be entitled to deduct a portion of the operating expenses and the depreciation on your home. To qualify for this deduction, the IRS stipulates that part of your home must be set aside *regularly* and *exclusively* for the business. In this regard, the space must be used as either (1) your principal place of business or (2) a place to meet and deal with patients, clients, or customers in the normal course of your business.

If your business occupies a free-standing structure next to your home—a studio, garage, or barn for example—its expenses are deductible if you use the space regularly and exclusively for the business. In this case, the structure does not have to be your principal place of business or used to meet customers.

If you have employees who work out of their homes they may be entitled to deduct expenses for the business use of their homes too. In this situation, though, they must work at home *for your convenience* and not just because it is appropriate and helpful in their jobs.

ABC ENTERPRISES
LIST OF DEPRECIABLE ASSETS

DATE	DESCRIPTION	COST	CLASS OF PROPERTY	DEPR. METHOD	DATE SOLD
1/16	TYPEWRITER	1250 00	8 yrs.		
2/15	AUTOMOBILE	11185 00	8 yrs.		
3/22	WORDPROCESSOR	3250 00	5 yrs.		
4/14	TELEPHONE ANSWERING DEVICE	225 00	5 yrs.		

Figuring Your Home Deduction

To figure what percentage of your home operating expenses and depreciation is deductible, use either of these two methods:

1. Divide the area used for your business by the total area of your home.

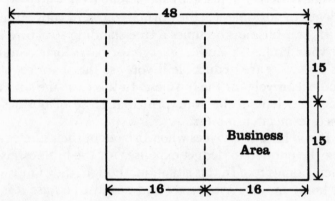

Business Area = 15×16 = 240 sq. ft.

$$\frac{240 \text{ sq. ft.}}{1200 \text{ sq. ft.}} = 20 \text{ percent}$$

Total Area = $\begin{array}{l} 15 \times 48 \\ + \\ 15 \times 32 \end{array}$ = 1200 sq. ft.

2. Divide the rooms used for your business by the number of rooms in your home.

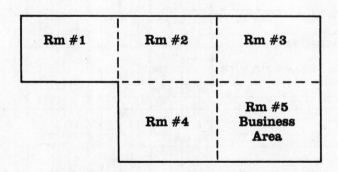

Business Rooms = $\dfrac{1}{5}$ = 20 percent

Total Rooms =

The second method is easier. In order for it to be accurate, though, all of the rooms in your home must be approximately the same size.

Once you've determined the percentage of your home expenses that is deductible, multiply this figure by each expense in order to obtain the dollar amounts of your deductions. (For example, 20 percent times a $1,000 home utilities expense equals a $200 business utilities expense.) Those expenses that benefit only your business, such as painting or remodeling the specific area occupied by the business, are 100 percent deductible. Expenses that benefit only your home and are in no way related to the business, such as lawn care and landscaping, may *not* be deducted.

To make certain you have accurately defined those expenses that benefit 1) both your home and your business, 2) only the business, and 3) only the home, it's advisable to consult with an accountant. This is especially important if you own rather than rent your home. If you decide to sell your home, the home expense deductions you've taken for the business will have a bearing on how and when capital gains on the sale are to be recognized. For more information on selling your home when a part of it is used as a business, check IRS publication number 523, "Tax Information on Selling Your Home."

Automobile Expenses

If you use an automobile or truck in your business, those expenses resulting from the business use of the vehicle are deductible. As stated in Chapter 1, this includes gasoline, oil, maintainance and repairs, insurance, depreciation, interest on car payments, parking fees, taxes, license fees, and tolls.

Calculating Your Automobile Expenses

There are two ways to calculate your deductible automobile expenses: (1) using a standard mileage rate, and (2) deducting a percentage of the total operating costs.

Standard Mileage Rate. To calculate your deductible expenses using this method, keep a record of all the miles you drive for business reasons during the year. Then multiply your total business mileage times the current rate allowed by the IRS. This will give you the dollar amount of your automobile expense:

> Business Miles
> × Standard Mileage Rate
> Automobile Expense (Parking fees and
> tolls may be added to this)

If you drive more than 15,000 business miles in any year, the standard mileage rate for each additional mile is reduced. Once you drive a vehicle 60,000 business miles, the standard mileage rate for all additional mileage for that vehicle drops again. The applicable rates are subject to change by the IRS.

Percentage of Total Operating Costs. To calculate your deductible expenses this way, keep a record of the number of miles you drive for business reasons during the year, *and* keep track of all of your automobile expenses. Then multiply the deductible percentage of automobile expenses times the total cost of operating your car:

$$\frac{12{,}000 \text{ Business Miles}}{20{,}000 \text{ Total Miles Driven}} = 60 \text{ percent}$$

> $5,000 Total Automobile Operating Costs
> × .60 Deductible Percentage
> $3,000 Automobile Expense (Parking Fees and tolls
> may be added to this)

Since this method is based on your automobile operating costs rather than on a standard rate per mile, it's especially important to keep receipts documenting your automobile expenses.

To make sure that you are claiming the full automobile deduction the IRS allows, you should try both of these methods (at least in the beginning). Then, after comparing the totals, choose the method that gives you the higher deduction.

Entertainment Expenses

Business entertainment expenses also are tax deductible. To qualify as a deductible item, the entertainment expense must be ordinary and necessary in carrying on your trade or operating your business. As with your home business expenses and automobile expenses, you must separate your business entertainment expenses from the nonbusiness ones. Whenever entertainment is for both business and social purposes, only the business part is deductible. For example, if you entertain a group that includes three business prospects and one social guest, you may deduct the expenses for yourself and the three prospects, but you may *not* deduct the amount you spend on the social guest.

In determining whether or not an entertainment expense is deductible, ask yourself if the entertainment had a clear business purpose. Was it to get new business or to encourage the continuation of an existing business relationship? If your answer is yes, then you should be able to claim the expense as a business deduction. For example, taking a prospective customer to lunch or dinner is a deductible expense if you discuss business at some time during the meal.

To comply with the IRS rules on entertainment deductions, you should keep a record of all business entertainment expenses along with the receipts or other supporting evidence to back them up. Entering a luncheon date on your desk calendar isn't enough. To be properly documented, the lunch must be backed up by the receipt for the meal.

When claiming an expense as a business entertainment deduction, you must be able to prove the following:

1. The amount of the expense
2. The date the entertainment took place
3. The location of the entertainment, such as a restaurant or theater
4. The reason for the entertainment (to make a sale, to discuss a business project)
5. The name and title (or occupation) of each person you entertained

The more specific you can be the better, since this will add to the validity of your deductions.

YOUR TAXES

Much as you might like to ignore them, taxes are an inevitable part of doing business. If you keep good records, taxes shouldn't pose a problem for you. The nature of your home-based business, its legal form, and its location will determine the taxes you must pay.

Federal Taxes

The two best-known federal taxes that home-based entrepreneurs are required to pay are income tax and self-employment tax. If you employ other people in your business or if you manufacture or sell certain types of goods, you may also be subject to employment taxes and excise taxes.

Income Tax

Every business is required by law to file an annual income tax return. The form you use for this depends on whether your business is a sole proprietorship, a partnership, or a corporation.

Sole Proprietorship. If you are a sole proprietor, you should report your business income and deductions on Schedule C (Form 1040). Attach this schedule to your individual tax return Form 1040 and submit them together. If you own more than one business, you must file a separate Schedule C for each one.

Partnership. If you are a partner in a home-based business, your income and deductions from the partnership should be reported on Schedule K-1 (Form 1065) and filed along with your individual tax return. Each of your partners should do the same, accounting for his or her income and deductions in this way. In addition to this, the total income and deductions for the partnership itself must be reported on Form 1065.

Corporation. A corporation reports its taxable income on Form 1120. S corporations use Form 1120S. Any income or dividends that you receive from the corporation should be entered on your individual tax return. However, if you are a shareholder in an S corporation, your income and deductions should be reported in the same way that they would be in a partnership. In this instance, though, you use Schedule K-1 (Form 1120S).

Self-Employment Tax

Self-employment tax is a Social Security tax for people who are self-employed. It's similar to the Social Security tax paid by wage earners, but you pay it yourself instead of having it withheld from your paycheck. As a home-based business-person, you must pay self-employment tax if you have net earnings from your business of $400 or more a year. To find out more about this tax, check IRS publication number 533, "Self-Employment Tax."

Estimated Tax

The IRS requires that you pay your income and self-employment taxes each year on a pay-as-you-go basis. Rather than paying them in one lump sum at the end of the tax period, you must estimate them in advance and pay them in installments by these dates:

- April 15
- June 15
- September 15
- January 15 (of the following year)

Using this method, you pay one-quarter of your total tax liability on each date until the liability is paid in full. If you discover in, say, August that you are paying too much or too little tax, you can decrease or increase the size of the remaining payments. Remember, though, that you are required to prepay at least 90 percent of your tax liability each year. If you prepay less than this, you may be subject to a penalty.

Try to make your estimates as accurate as possible to spare yourself that expense. When in doubt you will do better to pay more than the amount you've estimated so as to ensure meeting the 90 percent prepayment minimum. The form you use to estimate your tax is Form 1040-ES, which can be obtained from the IRS.

Employment Taxes

If you have employees in your home-based business, you will probably need to pay employment taxes. These taxes include:

1. Federal income tax, which you withhold from your employees' wages
2. Social Security tax, part of which you withhold from your employees' wages and the rest of which you contribute as an employer
3. Federal unemployment tax, which you as an employer must pay

Report both income tax and the Social Security tax on Form 941, and pay both taxes when you submit the forms. Report and pay the federal unemployment tax separately, using Form 940. For more information about employment taxes and which ones, if any, you must pay, read IRS publication number 15, "Circular E."

Excise Taxes

Any tax that is selective in nature, singling out some products or services for taxation but not others, is known as an excise tax. Although it's not likely that you will have to pay any excise taxes, you should be aware of their existence. Coming in a variety of categories, some excise taxes are levied on the production or sale of certain goods while others are imposed on specific kinds of services or businesses. For example, if your home-based business involves transporting people or property by air, it will be subject to an excise tax. If you are an insurance agent who handles policies issued by foreign insurers, you will have to pay excise taxes on those policies. If you manufacture, import, or sell fishing equipment, you may be liable for excise taxes.

As you can see, the subject of excise taxes is clearly a mixed bag. To determine whether your product, or service, or home-based business is subject to excise taxes, study IRS publication number 510, "Excise Taxes." This will give you the information you need about excise taxes, along with an explanation of the procedures for reporting them.

State and Local Taxes

The types and amounts of state and local taxes you, as a home-based business owner, must pay will depend on where your business is located. For instance, businesses in New York and California are subject to higher rates of taxation than those in Pennsylvania and Texas. Some states have income and sales taxes, whereas others don't. All states have unemployment taxes.

Just as the states vary when it comes to taxation, so do counties, cities, and towns within the states. Some of the taxes imposed at this level include business taxes, licensing fees, and income taxes.

To make sure that your business is meeting its state and local tax obligations, contact the authorities for your locality to determine those taxes for which you are responsible.

IRS TAX PUBLICATIONS

The publications listed below can provide you with additional information about business taxation. These publications should be available at your local IRS office; if not, you can obtain them by writing to the Internal Revenue Service, Washington, D.C. 20224.

TITLE	No.
Your Rights as a Taxpayer	1
The ABC's of Income Tax	2
Employer's Tax Guide (Circular E)	15

TITLE	No.
Your Federal Income Tax	17
Tax Guide for Small Business	334
Fuel Tax Credits and Refunds	378
Travel, Entertainment and Gift Expenses	463
Tax Withholding and Estimated Tax	505
Excise Taxes	510
Tax Information on Selling Your Home	523
Taxable and Nontaxable Income	525
Charitable Contributions	526
Residential Rental Property	527
Miscellaneous Deductions	529
Tax Information for Homeowners	530
Self-Employment Tax	533
Depreciation	534
Business Expenses	535
Accounting Periods and Methods	538
Tax Information on Partnerships	541
Tax Information on Corporations	542
Sale and Other Dispositions of Assets	544
Interest Expense	545
Nonbusiness Disasters, Casualties, and Thefts	547
Investment Income and Expenses	550
Basis of Assets	551
Recordkeeping for Individuals	552
Community Property and the Federal Income Tax	555
Examinations of Returns, Appeal Rights, and Claims for Refund	556
Self-Employed Retirement Plans	560
General Business Credit	572
Taxpayers Starting a Business	583
The Collection Process (Income Tax Accounts)	586A
Business Use of Your Home	587
Tax information on S Corporations	589
Individual Retirement Arrangements (IRAs)	590
Guide to Free Tax Services	910
Tax Information for Direct Sellers	911

TAX TIPS

1. Deposit all funds generated by your business in a bank account established just for the business.
2. Make all payments by check, rather than cash, so that your expenses are clearly documented.
3. Keep all business records and supporting documentation (checks, receipts, and other documents) at least three years.
4. Don't use your records only for tax purposes; the information contained in them is essential for decision-making too.
5. Choose the recordkeeping system that is most compatible with the needs of your business; for good measure, ask an accountant for advice *before* setting up your system.
6. If possible, require your customers to pay cash for their purchases, rather than collecting payment from them at a later date; this gives you the immediate use of the funds.
7. Keep a diary in your car and use it to record your automobile expenses, entering all business mileage and the purpose of each business trip.
8. Remember to document all business entertainment expenses; the easiest way to do this is to write the business information on the receipts themselves and keep them with your records.
9. To avoid a penalty, be sure to prepay 90 percent of your estimated income and Social Security taxes.
10. If you need to obtain tax forms in a hurry, check with your local library; even if the library is out of the forms, it may have samples that you can duplicate.

11

Safeguarding Your Business

THE same amount of effort you put into building your home-based business should also go into protecting it. What if a delivery person or a customer were hurt on your premises? Or a burglar broke into your home and stole your office equipment? A client decided to sue? You became ill or disabled and couldn't work? What would you do?

To deal with these and other hazards associated with working at home, it's important to take specific precautions. In essence, what's called for is an ongoing program of risk management.

RISK MANAGEMENT

An effective risk management program will enable you to cope with business risks in four ways—eliminating them, reducing them, accepting them, or transferring them.

Eliminating the Risk

Certain risks can and should be entirely eliminated. Among these are the risk of injury due to the use of inferior materials or poorly maintained equipment, the risk of fire because of frayed electrical cords or overloaded circuits, and the risk of neighborhood pollution because of inadequate waste-handling procedures. There's no excuse for allowing risks that are solely the result of negligence or indifference. You owe it to yourself and those around you to make your work environment as safe as possible.

Reducing the Risk

If a risk can't be eliminated, the next best thing is to reduce it. A carpenter or furniture craftsperson can't eliminate the risk of injury from a flying wood chip, but wearing safety goggles or other protective gear can reduce the risk. Properly storing toxic or flammable materials, such as artist's supplies and cleaning solvents, reduces the risk of them being misused. By installing an inexpensive surge suppressor on your computer line, you can guard your computer equipment and software against damages resulting from a sudden increase in electrical power. Consultants and others can reduce the risk of not getting paid for their work by running credit checks on new clients, insisting on written agreements, or requiring partial payment in advance.

Accepting the Risk

No matter how many safety measures you take, some minor business losses are bound to be incurred—inventory breakage or spoilage, returned merchandise, canceled appointments, or lost hours of work due to equipment breakdowns. Depending on what you anticipate these losses to be, you may decide to simply accept the risk, to cover the expenses out of your own pocket. However, you should accept, or assume, the risk in this way only when the risk can't be eliminated and buying insurance isn't cost-effective (i.e., the insurance premiums would exceed the covered loss).

When it comes to accepting risks, a word of caution is in order. Remember, losses that seem small at the outset sometimes have a way of ballooning in size later on, and you could wind up paying more than you planned.

Transferring the Risk

No risk management program would be complete without adequate insurance coverage. Purchasing insurance enables you to transfer the risk of loss to another party—the insurance company. In exchange for a fee, the insurance company agrees to accept those risks you wish to be protected against. In effect, when you transfer the risk to the insurer you're making the decision to absorb small periodic losses (premiums) rather than a large uncertain loss.

TYPES OF INSURANCE COVERAGE

Homeowner's Insurance

Since your business is at home, one of the first things you should do is check to see what kind of coverage, if any, is extended to the business under your homeowner's or renter's policy. For example, some policies cover business furnishings and equipment as a matter of course, including them with the rest of a home's contents. Other policies don't. Also, one policy may protect you from personal liability if a business visitor is injured in your home, while another policy won't.

It's important to find out what's covered and what's not. At the same time, you want to make sure that you don't inadvertently void your current policy by using your home to conduct business. Some homeowner's policies have a clause that forbids working at home. By notifying your insurance carrier early on, you can determine if your business activities are compatible with the terms of your policy. Then, depending on the circumstances, you can make the appropriate arrangements—updating, expanding, or replacing the policy as needed to obtain the amount of coverage you require.

Adding a "business option" rider to your existing homeowner's policy may be the answer. For a few dollars more per year, a business option typically reimburses you for damage or loss to business property and extends your homeowner's liability coverage to include business-related injuries. To find out more about this option and what it provides, talk to your insurance agent.

Even the most comprehensive homeowner's policy can't protect you against everything, though. In order to adequately safeguard yourself and your business, you should find out about the other kinds of insurance that are available and choose the coverage that suits your needs.

Automobile Insurance

If one or more automobiles or trucks will be used in your home-based business, automobile insurance is a must. This can protect you against property damage and bodily injury claims as well as the actions of uninsured motorists.

The amount of coverage you need and the cost of a policy depend on the number of cars or trucks being insured, their value, the kinds of driving they'll be used for (driving clients around, transporting materials and equipment), and your location. Just as with your homeowner's policy, you want to be careful not to void any existing automobile insurance you have by using your vehicles for work purposes without informing the insurer.

Liability Insurance

As a home-based businessperson, you're responsible for the safety of your customers and employees. You're also responsible for any injuries or damages that result from the products or services you sell.

To protect yourself accordingly, you may want to purchase one or more of the following types of liability insurance:

- *General liability insurance.* The most far-reaching type of liability insurance available, it provides basic coverage against all liabilities not specifically excluded from the policy.

- *Product liability insurance.* This insurance protects you against financial loss in the event that someone is injured by a product you manufacture or distribute.
- *Professional liability insurance.* For doctors, lawyers, consultants, and others who provide advice or information or perform a service, this insurance protects you against damages claims brought by dissatisfied clients.

Personal Insurance

Personal insurance protects both you and your employees, if any, against personal loss resulting from illness or injury. Health and life insurance, disability insurance, and worker's compensation all contribute to this protection.

Given the escalating costs of medical treatment, you can't afford not to have health insurance. If you are self-employed, one of your top priorities should be obtaining adequate and affordable health coverage. Some of the ways you can save money on health insurance include: (1) joining the group plan (if you qualify) of a company that employs your services, (2) being included on a spouse's insurance plan, (3) purchasing group insurance through a professional, trade, or fraternal association to which you belong.

To protect your continued earning power and ensure that your family's ongoing financial needs will be met, you may also want to buy disability insurance and life insurance. Again, if these aren't provided by an employer, then you should seriously consider them. In so doing, take the time to compare the various plans available, especially their "Ps"—premiums, provisions, and payouts—to get the best coverage.

If you employ others in your home-based business, you are required by law to have worker's compensation insurance to cover damages arising from on-the-job injuries or occupational diseases. In the event that an employee does become ill or injured, under worker's compensation the insurer pays all sums you are legally required to pay a claimant.

As your home-based business grows, you may also feel the need for *business interruption insurance* or *key personnel insurance*. The first would help to protect you against losses resulting from a temporary closure of your business due to a fire or some other disaster. The second would provide a buffer against the financial impact caused by the death or disability of a partner or key employee.

The best way to determine what types of insurance you should buy is to discuss your situation with an insurance professional. Then, working with your agent, you can put together an insurance package that fits your needs and budget.

ADDED SAFEGUARDS

When a property loss occurs it is the policy holder's responsibility to prove what the insured property was worth. Otherwise, payment on the claim could be delayed, reduced, or even denied by the insurance carrier.

To protect your right to the prompt handling and full payment of any claims you submit, make it a point to do the following:

- Save your receipt whenever you buy something new for the business.
- Prepare an inventory list describing the contents of your work area—furniture, equipment, merchandise, etc.— the date you bought each item, and what you paid for it. Note the serial number, too, if there is one since this will help to support your claim and can aid the police in recovering stolen property.
- Photograph or videotape the items on your inventory list. This will give police and insurance investigators even more to go on. And, if there is any question as to the value of the damaged or stolen property, the insurer can *see* what it looked like and the condition it was in.
- Keep your inventory list and photographs or videotape in a separate location—a safe deposit box, your accountant's office, etc. That way, if there is a theft or fire, they won't be lost or damaged.

- Take steps to lessen damages if you can, removing threatened property to a safe place whenever possible, covering broken windows after a burglary to prevent further losses, and so on. A failure to do this could result in the insurance company holding you partly responsible for the loss, thus jeopardizing your claim.
- Notify the insurance carrier as soon as possible after a loss occurs.
- Provide a detailed report of what happened, spelling out the nature and extent of the loss. The more thorough and accurate your account is, the easier it will be to collect on your claim.

INSURANCE TIPS

1. Identify existing hazards in your business; then try to eliminate or reduce them; an ounce of prevention *is* worth a pound of cure.
2. Don't risk voiding your homeowner's or renter's insurance policy by working at home without notifying the insurance carrier.
3. Analyze your personal and business situation to determine what kind of insurance coverage you need.
4. Talk to more than one insurance agent so that you can compare the various policies available.
5. Take advantage of any discounts you may qualify for, such as insurance policies written for nonsmokers, safe drivers, homeowners who equip their homes with smoke detectors, and so on.
6. Enroll in a group health insurance plan if possible, rather than taking out individual coverage; group plans generally offer better coverage at a lower price.
7. Look into the disability insurance offered by consumer credit companies; some companies now make this available to small business cardholders and their staffs as an added membership benefit.
8. Use an engraver's tool to inscribe your name and address on the backs of furniture, equipment, and other

belongings; if a theft occurs this will enable you to prove ownership of any recovered property.

9. Maintain a written and visual inventory of the possessions used in your home-based business; then keep it in a safe place so you'll have it when you need it.

10. Review your insurance policies periodically to make sure that the coverage they provide reflects your current needs.

12

Profiting from Your Personal Computer

COMPUTERS, modems, fax machines, and the like have become as much a part of the well-equipped home-based business as a phone and a filing cabinet. The "smart office" of the future is here today. Aided by an abundance of electronic gadgetry and services, home-based workers are maximizing their productivity and performing tasks once reserved for Big Business alone.

Given the sophisticated technology that's becoming increasingly available—and affordable—there's virtually no limit to what you can do from home. You can link up with government and commercial data banks to obtain information at the touch of a computer key; electronically send and receive letters, reports and documents; process words and "crunch" numbers; design graphics; maintain customer files and mailing lists; track inventory; transfer funds; oversee projects and work with clients—all without ever leaving your desk.

IDENTIFYING YOUR COMPUTER NEEDS

To make the most of the home office technology at your disposal, it's best to start out by identifying your computer needs. Based on the type of work you do, which computer applications would be of the greatest use to you?

- Word processing
- Accounting
- Financial analysis
- Database management
- Creating graphics
- Inventory control
- Purchasing
- Communications
- Planning

Once you've determined the tasks you would like a computer to perform, you can put together the system that matches your capability and cost requirements.

CHOOSING A COMPUTER SYSTEM

The first element you should consider in choosing your computer system is the software. The software (ready-made programs) is what ultimately enables the hardware (the computer itself and related equipment) to do the work. Since not all software is compatible with all hardware, if you buy the hardware beforehand you could end up with equipment that isn't able to run the programs you want.

Software

The number of business software packages on the market continues to grow along with the number of personal computers in use. Thousands of new programs are developed each year. So, in all likelihood, you should be able to find the software you need.

Some of the more popular business software packages are:

- *Word processing software*: enables you to produce error-free letters and other printed materials; edits text; checks spelling, grammar, and punctuation.
- *Spreadsheet software*: stores financial data and performs

mathematical calculations, assists in the preparation of accounting records and financial projections.

- *Database software*: organizes information on customers, suppliers, and inventory; manages mailing lists; and allows you to create personalized form letters and print address labels.
- *Graphics software*: turns your computer monitor into a drafting table or easel, giving you the ability to create detailed illustrations, logotypes, charts, maps, and graphs.
- *Communication software*: lets your computer interface with other computers and gain access to database information services, and facilitates office-to-office computing and file transfers via the telephone lines.
- *Project management software*: lets you keep track of projects, work in progress, billable hours and employees' output; handles billings and prepares invoices.

In making the decision to buy one software package or another, don't just rely on the word of the salesperson at the software store or go by the information on the box. Try out the program yourself to get a feel for it and what it can do.

The questions you should ask yourself are:

1. Does the program do what I want it to do?
2. How difficult is the program to use?
3. Is the price right?
4. Is the program compatible with my computer?
5. How much computer memory capacity will it take to operate the program?
6. Can I use the program with other programs I have?
7. What type of warranty comes with the package?
8. Will the manufacturer provide program updates ("enhancements") as they are developed?
9. Is the software documentation (instructions, training manual) well written and easy to understand?
10. Does the manufacturer have a toll-free number I can phone if I have questions?

Hardware

Once you've ascertained what software you'll be using, the next step is to assemble the equipment you will need to run it. Although equipment set-ups can have major differences in their size, complexity, or price, you'll find that their basic configurations are the same, consisting of these key elements: central processing unit (the "computer"), disk drives, keyboard, monitor, and printer.

Central Processing Unit (CPU). The computer itself, this is the "brain" of the system, the place where information is stored and work is carried out. Consisting of circuit boards containing arrangements of computer chips, the CPU is the most important hardware component in any system since it determines what you can do and how fast you can do it. The larger the CPU's memory, or storage capacity, the more functions it can perform. The greater the CPU's ability to route electronic impulses from one point to the next, the faster its computing speed.

Disk Drives. Disk drives enable you to transmit data back and forth between the CPU and magnetized storage disks used to augment the CPU's internal memory. Available in two versions—standard and "hard drive"—disk drives may be built into the framework housing the CPU or may be freestanding units. Standard disk drives accommodate small, flexible ("floppy") disks, usually 5¼ or 3½ inches across, which are inserted into the disk drive unit. Hard drives, on the other hand, have permanent disks contained within the unit that are capable of storing much greater amounts of information—the equivalent of hundreds of floppy disks.

Keyboard. An input device for entering data into the computer, a keyboard has the same keys found on a typewriter plus an assortment of extra "command" keys for transmitting instructions (to move a paragraph, center a heading, and so on). Although most keyboards look pretty much the same, there are some important features you should consider in comparing them. For instance, is the keyboard detachable from the computer? Can its angle of operation be adjusted to adapt to individual typing preferences? Do the keys respond well when you touch them? These factors will affect your comfort level when you're working at the computer. For best results, you should avoid rigid, inflexible keyboards or boards where the keys have a "mushy" feel to them. Also, if you plan to do a lot of "number crunching," make sure the keyboard has a built-in numeric pad with separate cursor controls.

Monitor. Basically a television screen, the monitor provides a visual display of the data being entered into the computer, thus enabling you to revise or organize files and read programming instructions. Monitors are available in either monochromatic (single-color) or color models. They also vary in the degree of picture resolution, or detail, they provide. Which you choose is largely a matter of personal preference. If you're working primarily with words or numbers, then a monochromatic monitor probably is best since single-color screens generally offer better resolution. On the other hand, if you're working with graphics, then a color monitor makes sense.

Printer. The printer allows you to take information from the computer and transfer it onto paper, creating a "hard copy." Printers range in price from low to high, with the most expensive being those that offer the best print quality and fastest printing times. The four basic types to choose from are:

- *Dot Matrix Printers*: The most commonly used printers because of their versatility and low prices, dot matrix printers operate by striking a sheet of paper with a set of tiny rods, or pins. Depending on the striking pattern, the pins can form letters and numbers or create graphics. The more pins the printer has, the finer the print quality. For "letter-quality" printing comparable to that done on a typewriter, you need a printer with 24 pins.
- *Daisy Wheel Printers*: Offering crisp, clean, letter-quality printing, daisy wheel printers function much the same way that a typewriter does. The symbols (letters, num-

bers, punctuation marks, etc.) that it types are all contained on interchangeable daisy wheels, which rotate, as directed, to strike the paper. Though perfect for typing correspondence or tabulating numbers, the daisy wheel printer's two main drawbacks are its slow speed and its inability to create graphics.

- *Inkjet Printers*: As the name implies, inkjet printers operate by spraying ink onto the paper to form the letters. Faster and quieter than both the dot matrix and daisy wheel printers, inkjet printers are especially good for creating graphics and printing first-draft copies. Lower-priced models generally lack the clarity to produce letter-quality printing, but the more expensive inkjet models are capable of doing so.

- *Laser Printers*: Offering the ultimate in print quality, versatility, and speed, laser printers use a laser beam to trace images on paper. The state of the art in computer printers, laser printers have proven invaluable to desktop publishers, graphic designers, engineers, and others who demand printing perfection. The only real drawbacks to the laser printer have been its high price, which until recently put it beyond the reach of most home-based workers, and its inability to accommodate continuous-feed paper or multi-copy forms.

Other Computer Hardware

Beyond the basic equipment just described, which is common to all computer systems, you may also want to use one or more of the following.

Modem. Once considered an exotic extra of interest only to dedicated hackers, the modem has come to be an integral part of many home-based workers' computer systems. Enabling a computer equipped with communication software to send and receive information over the telephone lines, a modem lets you plug into the world at large. With a modem you can work at home while staying on a corporate payroll ("telecommuting"), network with other computer users, connect with clients' computer systems, and access databases to obtain information or conduct business transactions.

Many personal computers now come equipped with internal modems that are already built into the computer. Otherwise, you can purchase a modem separately, choosing either an internal or an external model. In deciding what to buy make sure that the modem is compatible with the software you want to use and that it operates at a high enough speed (measured in "bauds") to send the kinds of data you plan to transmit.

Mouse. The mouse is a pointer-type device that lets you control the cursor and operate the computer without using the keyboard. Providing a "user-friendly" approach to computing, the mouse is particularly popular with computer novices and nontechnical people since it reduces the number of commands one must learn. Depending on the brand of equipment you buy, the mouse may be included in the price of the package. Or, just as with the modem, you can purchase one separately as an "add-on" item.

Track Ball. In considering the mouse you should also take a look at its relative, the *track ball.* Consisting of a ball mounted in a frame, the track ball activates the cursor and lets you draw pictures on the computer monitor by spinning the ball.

Plotter. If you need to produce high-quality, multicolor graphics, create architectural plans or engineering diagrams, or print on different types and sizes of surfaces (glossy paper, overhead transparencies, film, etc.) then you may want to add a plotter to your computer system. Specifically designed to produce graphics, plotters offer a rainbow of colors to choose from and can plot on a variety of surfaces. Using colored pens contained in the unit, plotters are especially suited for creating presentation-quality graphics in business reports and handouts and for creating technical drawings.

Scanner. One of the latest developments in personal computer technology is the scanner. Of particular use to desktop publishers, a scanner lets you convert printed matter —text, drawings, and photographs—into an electronic code that can be transmitted directly into your computer. Taking only seconds to scan a page, the scanner can significantly reduce the time spent on word processing or layout and pasteup work. Scanners are priced according to their reproduction capabilities. Color models cost more than black and white ones, just as high-resolution scanners cost more than those offering lower print quality.

In choosing the hardware components for your computer system, give each item a hands-on test before you buy.

At the same time, ask yourself:

1. What kind of work will I use it for in my business?
2. Which product features are most important to me?
3. Can the equipment operate the software packages I've selected?
4. Is it within my price range?
5. What kind of warranty comes with it?
6. What types of training and support will the manufacturer provide?
7. Is this something that will keep pace with my needs as my business grows?

FAX MACHINES

Just as computers have become a commonplace sight in home-based businesses, so have facsimile, or "fax," machines. Faster and cheaper than using express mail delivery service, a fax machine lets you transmit printed matter, artwork, or photographs to another fax machine in seconds. Delivery is just a telephone call away.

Available in a wide range of sizes, styles, and prices, fax machines are as versatile as they are ever-present. In addition to the basic office models, there are portable faxes that fit inside a briefcase, faxes designed for cellular car phones, and combination faxes that do double duty as telephone answering machines, printers, or scanners.

What you pay for a fax machine will depend on its transmission quality and features. Less expensive models may only transmit in black and white or a few shades of gray, while more expensive ones can send as many as 64 shades of gray. There are even fax machines on the market that can handle full color. If you're going to be sending drawings or photographs, make sure that the machine you choose is capable of transmitting at least 16 shades of gray. As for the different features that fax machines come with, these run the gamut from document feeders and built-in paper cutters to "autodialers" for automatic telephone dialing and electronic memories capable of storing pages of information for repeated transmissions.

As an alternative to buying a fax machine some people prefer to equip their computers with "fax modem boards." The fax board fits into a slot in your computer's CPU and lets you transmit data from your computer monitor to another computer or to a fax machine. With this you can also receive data back. On the plus side a fax modem is usually less expensive than a designated, stand-alone fax machine, and it has the advantage of transmitting information directly from the computer screen to the receiver. On the negative side the transmission quality isn't as good and you can only send data that is already entered into your computer. Possibly the biggest drawback, though, is in the area of receiving faxes. In order for the fax modem to work, your computer must be turned on at the time, thus requiring you to leave the computer on whether you're using it or not.

WAYS TO MAKE MONEY

In addition to being a useful tool in running a business, your computer can also help you make money by providing others with needed information or services.

Some of the computer-related businesses that are particularly suited for operating from home are:

- Billing services
- Bookkeeping and accounting
- Cataloguing services
- Communications specialist

- Computer consultant
- Computer dating service
- Computer programming
- Computer repair
- Data processing
- Desktop publishing
- Economics forecasting
- Editing
- Freelance writing
- Genealogy
- Graphic design
- Income tax preparation
- Investment counseling
- Mailing list brokers
- Mail order
- Management consulting
- Marketing research
- On-line databases
- Paralegal
- Personal shopping
- Polling services
- Private investigator
- Public relations
- Real estate sales
- Referral services
- Resume preparation
- Roommate bureaus
- Speakers bureaus
- Statistical analysis
- Technical writing
- Telemarketing
- Word processing

With a computer there's no end to the ways you can compete in the marketplace. More than any other recent invention, the personal computer has changed the face of business and, in so doing, provided untold opportunities to profit at home.

COMPUTER TIPS

1. Make sure that the hardware you buy is "expandable" (capable of being added onto or upgraded) so that your computer system can grow as your business needs grow.
2. Consider hiring a consultant to help you put together your computer system; you'll save money in the long run by avoiding costly mistakes and have someone to train you on the equipment.
3. Join a computer "users group" rather than going it alone; that way you'll have others to talk to when you have questions or need information.

4. Read computer magazines to stay on top of new developments in the computer field and how they might apply to your business.
5. Improve your computer skills by taking seminars at your local college or university.
6. When you're working on the computer be sure to back up your work as you go (every 5 to 10 minutes) to protect it against loss.
7. Remember, a computer is supposed to reduce your work, *not* create it; don't become so enamored of the technology at your disposal that you lose sight of its purpose and use the computer to perform unnecessary tasks.
8. During prolonged stretches on the computer take frequent minibreaks to reduce your levels of physical and mental fatigue.
9. Save your eyesight; if glare from the computer monitor is a problem, purchase a nonglare cover that fits over the screen.
10. Protect your computer equipment and software by keeping it out of direct sunlight and free from dust.

13

Resources

THE following resources should provide any additional information you may need to make your home-based business a success. Arranged alphabetically by type of business or occupation, these resource categories include books, directories, periodicals, and associations that you can refer to for guidance in starting and running your business.

If you have other questions or would like to contact us personally about your home-based business, write to us: Gregory and Patricia Kishel, P.O. Box 2967, Laguna Hills, CA 92654-2967. We would be delighted to hear from you.

ACCOUNTING/BOOKKEEPING

Financial Accounting Standards: Explanation and Analysis
Bill D. Jarnagin and Jon A. Booker
Commerce Clearing House, Inc., 4025 W. Peterson Avenue, Chicago, IL 60646

Income and Fees of Accountants in Public Practice
National Society of Public Accountants, 1010 N. Fairfax Street, Alexandria, VA 22134. Triennial

Managing Your Accounting and Consulting Practice
Mary Ann Altman and Robert I. Weil
Matthew Bender & Co., Inc., 11 Penn Plaza, New York,
NY 10017

Periodicals

Journal of Accountancy
American Institute of Certified Public Accountants, 1211
Avenue of the Americas, New York, NY 10036

National Public Accountant
National Society of Public Accountants, 1010 N. Fairfax
Street, Alexandria, VA 22314

Associations

American Institute of Certified Public Accountants
1211 Avenue of the Americas, New York, NY 10036

National Society of Public Accountants
1010 North Fairfax Street, Alexandria, VA 22314

ADVERTISING AGENCIES

Advertising Agency Business
Herbert S. Gardner
National Textbook Co., 4255 W. Touhy Avenue, Lincoln-
wood, IL 60646

Handbook of Advertising and Marketing Services
Executive Communications Inc., 919 Third Avenue, New
York, NY 10022. Biennial

Standard Directory of Advertising Agencies
National Register Publishing Co., 3004 Glenwood Road,
Wilmette, IL 60091. Annual

Periodicals

AD DAY/USA
A.S.M. Communications, 49 E. 21st Street, New York, NY
10010

Advertising Age
220 E. 42nd Street, New York, NY 10017.

Adweek
49 E. 21 Street, New York, NY 10010

Association

American Association of Advertising Agencies
666 Third Avenue 13th Floor, New York, NY 10017

AGRIBUSINESS

Agricultural Finance
Warren F. Lee and others
Iowa State University Press, 2121 S. State Avenue, Ames,
  IA 52244

Agricultural Guide to Washington: Whom to Contact and Where
Elanco Products Co., Lilly Corporate Center, Indianapolis,
  IN 46285. Free

Farm Management: Principles, Budgets, Plans
John Herbst
Stipes Publishing Co., 10–12 Chester Street, Champaign,
  IL 61820

Periodical

Kiplinger Agricultural Letter
Kiplinger Washington Editors, Inc. 1729 H. Street, Washington, D.C. 20006

Associations

Agriculture Council of America
1250 I Street, N.W., Suite 601, Washington, D.C. 20005

American Society of Agricultural Consultants
8301 Greensboro Drive, Suite 260, McLean, VA 22102

ANIMAL/PET CARE

Pet Dealer Annual Purchasing Guide Issue
567 Morris Avenue, Elizabeth, NJ 07208. Annual

Periodicals

Pet Age
207 S. Wabash Avenue, Chicago, IL 60604

Pet Dealer
567 Morris Avenue, Elizabeth, NJ 07208

Pets, Supplies, Marketing
Harcourt Brace Jovanovich, Inc. 7500 Old Oak Boulevard,
   Cleveland, OH 44130

Association

National Retail Pet Store and Groomers Association
711 Mission Street, Suite B, South Pasadena, CA 91030

ANTIQUES

*How to be Successful in the Antique Business: A Complete Guide
   to Opening and Running Your Own Antique Shop*
Ronald S. Barlow
Charles Scribner's Sons, 866 3rd Avenue, New York, NY
   10022

Selling Collectibles for Profit and Capital Gain
Richard Rush
Harper and Row Publishers, Inc., 10 E. 53rd Street, New
   York, NY 10022

Periodicals

The Antique Trader Weekly
P.O. Box 1050, Dubuque, IA 52001

The Magazine Antiques
980 Madison Avenue, New York, NY 10021

APPLIANCE REPAIR

Periodical

Appliance Service News
Gamit Enterprises, Inc., 110 W. Saint Charles Road, Box
  789, Lombard, IL 60148

Association

National Appliance Service Association
406 W. 34th Street, Suite 628, Kansas City, MO 64111

ARCHITECTURE/ENGINEERING

Architects Handbooks of Professional Practice
American Institute of Architects, 1735 New York Avenue,
  N.W., Washington, D.C. 20006

Marketing Architectural and Engineering Services
Weld Coxe
Van Nostrand Reinhold Co., Inc., 115 Fifth Avenue, New
  York, NY 10003

*Success Strategies for Design Professionals: Superpositioning for
  Architects and Engineering Firms*
Weld Coxe
McGraw-Hill, 420 N. Cascade Avenue, Colorado Springs,
  CO 80903

Periodical

Architecture
American Institute of Architects, 1735 New York Avenue,
  N.W., Washington, D.C. 20006

Association

American Institute of Architects
1735 New York Avenue, N.W., Washington, D.C. 20006

BED AND BREAKFASTS/INNS

Managing Front Office Operations
Charles E. Steadmon
Educational Institute of the American Hotel & Motel Association, P.O. Box 1240, East Lansing, MI 48823

The Bed and Breakfast Directory
Barbara Notarius
John Wiley & Sons, 605 Third Avenue, New York, N.Y. 10158

Associations

American Bed and Breakfast Association
16 Village Green, Suite 203, Cotton, MD 21114

Tourist House Association of American
R.D. 2, Box 355A, Greentown, PA 18426

BEAUTY/COSMETICS

Cosmetology
Jack Rudman
National Learning Corp., 212 Michael Drive, Syosset, NY 11791

Periodical

American Salon
Harcourt Brace Jovanovich, 7500 Old Oak Boulevard, Cleveland, OH 44130

Association

National Cosmetologists Association
3510 Olive Street, St. Louis, MO 63103

CARPENTRY/PLUMBING

Carpentry and Building Construction
John Feirer
Macmillan Publishing Co., 866 Third Avenue, New York,
NY 10022

Plumbers Handbook
Howard C. Massey
Craftsman Book Co., P.O. Box 6500, Carlsbad, CA 92008

Periodicals

Carpenter
101 Constitution Avenue, N.W., Washington, D.C. 20001

Plumbing Engineer
135 Addison Avenue, Elmhurst, IL 60126

Association

United Brotherhood of Carpenters and Joiners of America
101 Constitution Ave., N.W. Washington, D.C. 20001

CATERERS AND CATERING

Catering Handbook
Hal Weiss and Edith Weiss
J. Williams Book Co., P.O. Box 783, Jenks, OK 74037

Successful Catering
Bernard R. Splaver
Van Nostrand Reinhold Co., Inc., 115 Fifth Avenue, New
York, NY 10003

Periodical

Cooking for Profit
Metanoia Corp., Box 267, Fond Du Lac, WI 54935

Association

International Food Service Executive's Association
3017 W. Charleston Boulevard, Suite 50, Las Vegas, NV
    89102

CLEANING

Everything You Need to Know to Start a House Cleaning Service
Mary P. Johnson
Cleaning Consultants Services, Inc., 1512 Western Ave-
    nue, Seattle, WA 98101

CLIPPING BUREAU

Starting and Operating a Clipping Service
Demaris C. Smith
Pilot Books, 103 Cooper Street, Babylon, NY 11702

CLOTHING/FASHIONS

Buyer's Guide to the New York Market
Earnshaw Publications, Inc., 225 W. 34th Street, Rm. 212,
    New York, NY 10122. Annual

Convention Yearbook
International Association of Clothing Designers, 450 Sev-
    enth Avenue, New York, NY 10123

Directory of Men's and Boys' Wear Specialty Stores
Lebhar-Friedman, Inc., 425 Park Avenue, New York, NY
    10022. Annual

Drawing and Designing Children's and Teenage Fashions
Patrick J. Ireland
Halsted Press, 605 Third Avenue, New York, NY 10158

Periodicals

Apparel Industry Magazine
Shore Publishing Co., 180 Allen Road, N.E., Atlanta, GA
    30328

WWD: The Retailer's Daily Newspaper
Fairchild Publications, Seven E. 12th Street, New York,
   NY 10003

Associations

American Apparel Manufacturers Association
2500 Wilson Boulevard, Suite 301, Arlington, VA 22201

Clothing Manufacturers of the U.S.A.
1290 Avenue of the Americas, Suite 1061, New York, NY
   10104

COMPUTERS

Personal Computer Applications
Bryan Pfaffenberger
Scott Foresman & Co., 1900 E. Lake Avenue, Glenview,
   IL 60025

Software Encyclopedia
R. R. Bowker Co., 245 W. 17th Street, New York, NY
   10011. Annual

SpecCheck Personal Computer Guide
Dataquest, Inc., 1290 Ridder Park Drive, San Jose, CA
   95131. Semiannual

Using Computers
D. G. Dologite
Prentice-Hall, Inc., Rte. 9 West, Englewood Cliffs, NJ
   07632

Periodicals

Byte
Byte Publications, One Phoenix Mill Lane, Peterborough,
   NH 03458

PC Computing, America's Computing Magazine
Ziff-Davis Publishing Co.
4 Cambridge Center,
Cambridge, MA 02142

Association

Associations of Electronic Cottagers
P.O. Box 1738, Davis, CA 95617

CONSULTANTS

Cashing in on the Consulting Boom
Gregory F. Kishel and Patricia G. Kishel
John Wiley & Sons, Inc., 605 Third Avenue, New York,
   NY 10158

Managing Your Accounting and Consulting Practice
Mary Ann Altman and Robert I. Weil
Matthew Bender & Co., Inc., 11 Penn Plaza, New York,
   NY 10017

Periodical

Consulting News
Kennedy & Kennedy, Inc., Templeton Road, Fitzwilliam,
   NH 03447

Associations

ACME Inc.
The Association of Management Consulting Firms, 230
   Park Avenue, New York, NY 10169

American Consulting Engineers Council
1015 15th Street, N.W., Washington, D.C. 20005

Association of Managing Consultants
19 W. 44th Street, Suite 810, New York, NY 10036

DAY-CARE CENTERS

Day Care Centers for Children: A Bibliography
Day Care Centers for the Elderly: A Bibliography
Mary Vance
Vance Bibliographies, P.O. Box 229, Monticello, IL 61856

Periodical

Day Care Center
P.O. Box 249, Cobalt, CT 06414

DOLLS/MINIATURES

The Market for Collectible Dolls
FIND/SVP, 625 Avenue of the Americas, New York, NY
 10011

Periodicals

Dolls—The Collector's Magazine
170 Fifth Avenue, New York, NY 10010

The Miniature Collector
Collector Communications, 170 Fifth Avenue, New York,
 NY 10010

Associations

International Foundation of Doll Makers
P.O. Box 14438, Fort Worth, TX 76117

Miniatures Industry Association of America
P.O. Box 2188, Zanesville, OH 43702

ELECTRONICS REPAIR

Color and Black and White Television Theory and Servicing
Alvin Liff
Prentice-Hall, Inc., Route 9 West, Englewood Cliffs, NJ
 07632

Periodical

Electronic Servicing & Technology
Intertec Publishing Corp., 9221 Quivira Rd., Overland
 Park, KS 66212

Association

National Electronic Sales and Service Dealers Association
2708 W. Berry Street, Fort Worth, TX 76109

EMPLOYMENT AGENCIES

Employment Agency Law: A Guide for the Personnel Professional
A. Bernard Frechtman
National Association of Personnel Consultants, 1432 Duke
    Street, Alexandria, VA 22314

Periodical

Recruiting Trends: The Monthly Newsletter for Recruiting Executives
Enterprise Publications, 20 N. Wacker Drive, Chicago, IL
    60606

Associations

National Association of Personnel Consultants
1432 Duke Street, Alexandria, VA 22314

National Association of Temporary Services
119 S. Saint Asaph Street, Alexandria, VA 22314

EXPORT-IMPORT TRADE

Customs Regulations of the United States
U.S. Bureau of Customs
U.S. Government Printing Office, Washington, DC 20402

Exporting from the U.S.A.
Self-Counsel Press, Inc., 1704 N. State Street, Bellingham,
    WA 98225

The Financing of Exports and Imports: A Guide to Procedures
Morgan Guaranty Trust Co. of New York, 23 Wall Street,
    New York, NY 10005. Free

U.S. Import Trade Regulation
Eugene T. Rossides
Bureau of National Affairs, Inc., 1231 25th Street, N.W.,
  Washington, DC 20037.

Periodicals

International Trade Alert
American Association of Exporters and Importers, 11 W.
  42nd Street, New York, NY 10036

Journal of Commerce Import Bulletin
Journal of Commerce, 110 Wall Street, New York, NY
  10005

Association

American Association of Exporters and Importers
11 W. 42nd Street, New York, NY 10036

FLORIST

Retail Florist Business
Peter B. Pfahl and P. Blair Pfahl, Jr.,
Interstate Printers & Publishers, Inc., P.O. Box 50, Dan-
  ville, IL 61834

Periodical

Flowers
Barbara Cady
Teleflora, Inc., 12233 W. Olympic Boulevard, Suite 260,
  Los Angeles, CA 90064

Association

Society of American Florists
1601 Duke St., Alexandria, VA 22314

FOOD

Almanac of the Canning, Freezing, Preserving Industries
Edward E. Judge and Sons, Inc., P.O. Box 866, Westminister, MD 21157. Annual

Candy Marketer—Buyer's Directory Issue
Harcourt Brace Jovanovich, 7500 Old Oak Boulevard, Cleveland, OH 44130. Annual.

Foods and Food Production Encyclopedia
Douglas M. Considine and Glenn D. Considine
Van Nostrand Reinhold Co., Inc., 115 Fifth Avenue, New York, NY 10003

FURNITURE AND WOODWORKING

Advanced Woodwork and Furniture Making
John L. Feirer and Gilbert R. Hutchings
Charles Scribner's Sons, 866 Third Avenue, New York, NY 10022

Woodworking Factbook: Basic Information on Wood for Wood Carvers, Home Woodshop Craftsmen, Tradesmen and Instructors
Donald G. Colemen
Robert Speller and Sons Publishers, Inc., P.O. Box 411, Madison Square Station, New York, NY 10159

Periodical

Furniture Design and Manufacturing
Delta Communications, Inc., 400 N. Michigan, 13th Floor, Chicago, IL 60611

GIFT BUSINESS

Gift and Stationery Business
Gralla Publications, 1515 Broadway, New York, NY 10036. Annual

Salesman's Guide Nationwide Directory: Gift and Housewares and Stationery Buyers
Salesman's Guide, 1140 Broadway, New York, NY 10001

Periodical

Giftware News
Talcott Communications Corp., 1414 Merchandise Mart, Chicago, IL 60654

Association

Gift Association of America
1511 K Street, N.W., Suite 716, Washington, D.C. 20005

GREETING CARDS

Periodical

Greetings
Mackay Publishing Corp., 309 Fifth Avenue, New York, NY 10016

Association

Greeting Card Association
1350 New York Avenue, N.W., Suite 615, Washington, D.C. 20005

INSURANCE AGENTS

Responsibilities of Insurance Agents and Brokers
Bertram Harnett
Matthew Bender & Co., Inc., 11 Penn Plaza, New York, NY 10017

Periodical

Independent Agent
100 Church Street, New York, NY 10007

Association

Professional Insurance Agents
400 N. Washington Street, Alexandria, VA 22314

INTERIOR DESIGN

How to Make More Money at Interior Design
Robert Alderman
Interior Design Books, 249 W. 17th Street, New York, NY
   10011

Interior Decorators' Handbook
Columbia Communications, Inc., 370 Lexington Avenue,
   New York, NY 10017. Semiannual

Periodicals

Interior Design
Cahners Publishing Co., 249 W. 17th Street, New York,
   NY 10011

Interiors
Billboard Publications, Inc., 1515 Broadway, New York,
   NY 10036

Association

American Society of Interior Designers
1430 Broadway, New York, NY 10018

INVENTIONS

*Inventor's Guide in a Series of Four Parts: How to Protect,
   Search, Compile Facts and Sell Your Invention*
Chester L. Cook
C.L. Cook, P.O. Box 1511, Slidell, LA 70458

The Practical Inventor's Handbook
Orville Greene and Frank Durr
McGraw-Hill Book Co., 1221 Avenue of the Americas,
   New York, NY 10020

Associations

American Society of Inventors
P.O. Box 58426, Philadelphia, PA 19102

Inventors Workshop International Education
3201 Corte Malpaso, Suite 304-A, Camarillo, CA 93010

JEWELRY

Handbook of Jewelry Store Management
Jewelers' Book Club, Chilton Way, Radnor, PA 19080

Watch and Clock Making and Repairing
W.J. Gazeley
Van Nostrand Reinhold Co., Inc., 135 W. 50th Street, New
York, NY 10020

Periodicals

American Jewelry Manufacturer
Chilton Book Co., Chilton Way, Radnor, PA 19089

Jewelry Making, Gems and Minerals
Gemac Corp., c/o Jewelers Bench, Box 226, Cortaro, AZ
85652

National Jeweler
Gralla Publications, 1515 Broadway, New York, NY 10036

Associations

American Gem Society
5901 W. Third Street, Los Angeles, CA 90036

Gemological Institute of America
1660 Stewart Street, Santa Monica, CA 90404

Jewelry Manufacturers Association
475 Fifth Avenue, New York, NY 10017

LANDSCAPE ARCHITECTURE

Periodicals

Landscape Architecture
American Society of Landscape Architects, 1733 Connecticut Avenue, N.W., Washington, D.C. 20009

Landscape Industry
Brantwood Publications, Inc., Northwood Plaza Station, Clearwater, FL 33519

Association

American Society of Landscape Architects
1733 Connecticut Avenue, N.W., Washington, D.C. 20009

LAWYERS

ABA/BNA Lawyer's Manual on Professional Conduct
Bureau of National Affairs, Inc., 1231 25th Street, N.W., Washington, D.C. 20037

How to Manage Your Law Office
Mary Ann Altman and Robert I. Weil
Matthew Bender & Co., Inc., 11 Penn Plaza, New York, NY 10017

Relative Values: Determining Attorneys' Fees
Legal Procedures, Inc., Shepard's/McGraw-Hill, 420 N. Cascade Avenue, Colorado Springs, CO 80901

Periodicals

American Bar Association Journal
American Bar Association, 750 N. Lake Shore Drive, Chicago, IL 60611

Law Office Economics and Management
Callaghan & Co., 155 Pfingsten Road, Deerfield, IL 60015

Association

American Bar Association
750 N. Lake Shore Drive, Chicago, IL 60611

MAIL ORDER

Directory of Mailing List Houses
B. Klein Publications, Inc., P.O. Box 8503, Coral Springs,
  FL 33065

Sell it by Mail: Making Your Product the One They Buy
J. E. A. Lumley
John Wiley & Sons, Inc., 605 Third Avenue, New York,
  NY 10158

Periodicals

Catalog Marketer
Maxwell Sroge Publishing, 228 N. Cascade Avenue, Colorado Springs, CO 80903

Direct Marketing Magazine
Hoke Communications, Inc., 224 Seventh Street, Garden City, NY 11530

Associations

Direct Marketing Association
Six E. 43rd Street, New York, NY 10017

National Mail Order Association
5818 Venice Boulevard, Los Angeles, CA 90019

MUSIC

Billboard Guide to Music Publicity
James Pettigrew
Watson-Guptill, One Astor Plaza, 1515 Broadway, New York, NY 10036

Entertainment, Publishing and the Arts Handbook
John D. Viera and Robert Thorne
Clark Boardman Co., Ltd., 435 Hudson Street, New York,
NY 10014. Annual

Music and Booking Source Directory
6525 Sunset Boulevard, Studio A, Hollywood, CA 90028.
Annual

Periodical

Billboard
Billboard Publications, Inc., One Astor Plaza, 1515 Broadway, New York, NY 10036

NEW PRODUCTS

Venture Product News
General Electric Co., Technology Marketing Operation,
120 Erie Boulevard, Schenectady, NY 12305. Annual

Periodical

International New Product Newsletter
6 St. James Avenue, Boston, MA 02116

NUTRITION

Periodicals

Health Foods Business
Howmark Publishing Corp. Inc., 567 Morris Avenue, Elizabeth, NJ 07208

Nutrition Health Review
171 Madison Avenue, New York, NY 10016

Associations

American Dietetic Association
216 W. Jackson Boulevard, Suite 800, Chicago, IL 60606

National Nutritional Foods Association
125 E. Baker Street, Suite 230, Costa Mesa, CA 92626

PHOTOGRAPHY

Photographer's Market: Where to Sell Your Photos
Writer's Digest Books, 1507 Dana Avenue, Cincinnati, OH
   45207. Annual

Periodicals

Modern Photography
825 Seventh Avenue, New York, NY 10019

Professional Photographer
Professional Photographers of America, 1090 Executive
   Way, Des Plaines, IL 60018

Associations

National Free Lance Photographers Association
Box 629, Doylestown, PA 18901

Professional Photographers of America
1090 Executive Way, Des Plaines, IL 60018

PUBLIC SPEAKING

Public Speaking
Wayne C. Minnick
Houghton Mifflin Co., One Beacon Street, Boston, MA
   02108

Periodical

Quote
Box 3157, Sidell, LA 70459

Associations

National Speakers Association
3877 N. Seventh Street, Suite 350, Phoenix, AZ 85014

Toastmasters International
2200 N. Grand Avenue, P.O. Box 10400, Santa Ana, CA 92711

PUBLISHING

Book Marketing Handbook: Tips and Techniques
Nat G. Bodian
R. R. Bowker, 245 W. 17th Street, New York, NY 10011

Desktop Publishing by Design
Ronnie Shushan and Don Wright
Microsoft Press, 16011 N.E. 36th Way, Redmond, WA 98073

Periodicals

Publish! The How-To Magazine of Desktop Publishing
PCW Communications, Inc. 501 Second St., San Francisco, CA 94107

Publishers Weekly
R. R. Bowker Co., 245 W. 17th Street, New York, NY 10011

Associations

American Booksellers Association
137 W. 25th Street, New York, NY 10001

National Association of Desktop Publishers
P.O. Box 508, Kenmore Station, Boston, MA 02215

Newsletter Association
1401 Wilson Boulevard, Suite 403, Arlington, VA 22209

Women's National Book Association
160 Fifth Avenue, Room 604, New York, NY 10010

REAL ESTATE

Analyzing Real Estate Opportunities: Market and Feasibility Studies
Stephen Messner and Bryl Boyce
Prentice-Hall, Inc., Route 9 West, Englewood Cliffs, NJ 07632

Real Estate Brokerage: A Success Guide
John E. Cyr and Joan Sobeck
Longman Financial Services Institute, Inc., 520 N. Dearborn Street, Chicago, IL 60610

Periodicals

Journal of Property Management
Institute of Real Estate Management, Box 109025, Chicago, IL 60610

Real Estate Today
National Association of Realtors, 430 N. Michigan Avenue, Chicago, IL 60611

Associations

Apartment Owners and Managers Association of America
65 Cherry Avenue, Watertown, CT 06795

National Association of Realtors
430 N. Michigan Avenue, Chicago, IL 60611

RETAIL TRADE

Fairchild's Financial Manual of Retail Stores
Fairchild Publications, Seven E. 12th Street, New York, NY 10003. Annual

Retailing Principles and Practices
Dale Lewison and Wayne Delozier
Charles E. Merrill Publishing Co., 1300 Alum Creek Drive, Columbus, OH 43216

Periodical

Retailing Today
Robert Kahn and Associates, P.O. Box 249, Lafayette, CA
  94549

Association

National Retail Merchants Associations
100 W. 31st Street, New York, NY 10001

SALESMANSHIP

How to Sell Effectively
Extension Institute, American Management Association,
  135 W. 50th Street, New York, NY 10020

Periodical

Opportunity Magazine
Six N. Michigan Avenue, Chicago, IL 60602

SECRETARIAL SERVICES

Complete Secretary's Handbook
Lillian Doris and Bessie M. Miller
Prentice-Hall, Inc., Route 9 West, Englewood Cliffs, NJ
  07632

Notary Public Practices and Glossary
Raymond C. Rothman
National Notary Association, 8236 Remmet Avenue, P.O.
  Box 7184, Canoga Park, CA 91304

Résumé Writing
Burdette E. Bostwick
John Wiley & Sons, Inc., 605 Third Ave., New York, NY
  10158

Periodicals

The Answer
Associated Telephone Answering Exchanges, 320 King Street, Suite 500, Alexandria, VA 22314

Secretary
301 E. Armour Boulevard, Kansas City, MO 64111

Associations

Association of Telemessaging Services International
320 King Street, Suite 300, Alexandria, VA 22314

Professional Secretaries International
301 E. Armour Boulevard, Kansas City, MO 64111

STOCK BROKERS

Audits of Brokers and Dealers in Securities
American Institute of Certified Public Accountants, 1211 Avenue of the Americas, New York, NY 10036

National Association of Securites Dealers Manual
Commerce Clearing House, Inc., 4025 W. Peterson Avenue, Chicago, IL 60646. Annual

Periodical

Registered Representatives
Plaza Publishing Co., 18818 Teller Avenue, No. 280, Newport Beach, CA 92715

Association

National Association of Securities Dealers
1735 K Street, N.W., Washington, D.C. 20006

TELEMARKETING

How to Sell Successfully by Phone
Ken T. Peterson
Dartnell Corp. 4660 Ravenswood Avenue, Chicago, IL
    60640

Total Telemarketing
Robert McHatton
John Wiley & Sons, Inc., 605 Third Avenue, New York,
    NY 10158

Association

American Telemarketing Association
5000 Van Nuys Boulevard, No. 400, Sherman Oaks, CA
    91403

TOYS AND GAMES

Official Toy Directory
Edgell Communications, 545 Fifth Avenue, New York, NY
    10017. Annual

Periodicals

Games
810 Seventh Avenue, New York, NY 10019

Playthings
Geyer-McAllister Publications, 51 Madison Avenue, New
    York, NY 10010

Toy and Hobby World
International Thompson Retail Press, Inc., 345 Park Av-
    enue South, New York, NY 10010

Associations

Toy Manufacturers of America
200 Fifth Avenue, New York, NY 10010

Toy Wholesalers Association of America
66 E. Main Street, Morristown, NJ 08507

TRADE SHOWS

How to Participate Profitably in Trade Shows
Robert B. Konokow
Dartnell Corp., 4660 Ravenswood Avenue, Chicago, IL
  60640

Trade Show and Professional Exhibits Directory
Gale Research Co., Book Tower, Detroit, MI 48226

Association

International Exhibitors Association
5103-B Blacklick Road, Annandale, VA 22003

TRAVEL AND TOURS

ICTA Travel Management Text Series
Institute of Certified Travel Agents, 148 Linden Street,
  Wellesley, MA 02181

Periodical

ASTA Agency Management
666 Fifth Avenue, New York, NY 10013

Associations

American Society of Travel Agents
1101 King Street, Alexandria, VA 22314

United States Tour Operators Association
211 East 51st Street, Suite 12B, New York, NY 10022

WORD PROCESSING

All About Word Processing Software Packages
Datapro Research Corp., 1805 Underwood Boulevard,
  Delran, NJ 08075. Annual

Creative Word Processing
Vivian Dubrovin
Franklin Watts, Inc., 387 Park Avenue South, New York, NY 10016

Periodical

TypeWorld: The Newspaper for Electronic Publishing
Typesetting and Graphic Communications, Box 170, Salem, NH 03079

Association

National Association of Professional Word Processing Technicians
110 W. Byberry Road (E-2), Philadelphia, PA 19116

WRITING

Writer's Handbook
Writer, Inc., 120 Boylston Street, Boston, MA 02116. Annual

Writer's Market: Where to Sell What You Write
Writer's Digest Books, 1507 Dana Avenue, Cincinnati, OH 45207. Annual

Periodicals

Freelance Writer's Report
Cassell Communications Inc., P.O. Box 9844, Fort Lauderdale, FL 33310

The Writer
The Writer Publishers, 120 Boylston Street, Boston, MA 02116

Writer's Digest
P.O. Box 2124, Harlan, IA 51593

Associations

Authors Guild
234 W. 44th Street, New York, NY 10036

PEN American Center
568 Broadway, New York, NY 10012

Index